*"This gorgeous book is a must for anyone who has been fortunate
enough to spend time at Nick's Cove. Dena's heartfelt words
and Frankie's stunning images capture the extraordinary
history and contemporary luxury that is Nick's. The recipes
are so compelling, you'll want to cook through the entire
book—many are destined to become family traditions."*

— GIBSON THOMAS
publisher and editor, *Edible Marin & Wine Country*

*"This cookbook honors my family's legacy and the history of
Nick's Cove, and it recognizes the importance of tradition."*

—JUDI MATKOVICH RITZ
daughter of former owners of Nick's Cove

TABLE WITH A VIEW

THIS BOOK IS DEDICATED TO MY
NAVIGATOR FOR LIFE, PRESCOTT ASHE.

EVERY SUNSET BELONGS TO YOU.

TABLE WITH A VIEW

THE HISTORY & RECIPES OF NICK'S COVE

Dena Grunt

photography by Frankie Frankeny
recipes edited by chef Kua Speer

CAMERON + COMPANY
Petaluma, California

CONTENTS

MAIN COURSES

SWEETS

COCKTAILS

INTRODUCTION

Whether you've visited once or have spent so many weekends at Nick's Cove that you've lost count, it's hard not to be swept away by the beauty of this bayside getaway. From the moment I saw it, years before I began working there, I knew that Nick's Cove was destined to become a big part of my life.

In October 1992, while living in Petaluma, I met Hans Grunt, "the boy next door," who would later become my husband. Throughout our years of dating, I heard stories of his adventures as a kid in West Marin and Tomales Bay. I grew to understand how the area came to hold a very special place in his heart. And loving him meant it would come to have a special place in my heart, too. I enthusiastically listened to Hans's tales of his somewhat fanciful (and minimally adult-supervised) childhood.

The summer Hans turned fifteen, he worked for the son of Ed Holly, a local who, at the time, owned a pier and boat repair on Highway 1 in the small town of Marshall. Hans had been hired to help upgrade a fishing boat that, on the heels of the blockbuster movie *Jaws*, had been contracted to catch a great white shark live for SeaWorld in Southern California. He also told me about a "really cool," no-frills roadside spot where he, his dad, and his brother would regularly grab burgers: Nick's Cove.

Hans has always had a love affair with Tomales Bay, so it should come as no surprise that on June 16, 1996, sometime after taking off from Blue Waters Kayak, just south of Nick's Cove, for a day of kayaking on the bay, we stopped at the

small, picturesque Hog Island and went ashore. There, he dropped to one knee and proposed.

Living in Petaluma, Hans and I often spent our weekends hiking in Point Reyes National Seashore and perusing the shops in Point Reyes Station. We always stopped at Bovine Bakery for one of their perfect scones, and many date nights were spent at Tony's Seafood on Highway 1. So much of our relationship history took place in West Marin that, in 2007, when we heard that Nick's Cove had been beautifully restored and reopened, we were excited to try this new destination in our favorite area.

We set out on a dark and stormy night, and although the rain was heavy, we made our way to Nick's Cove with confidence, having driven the twists and turns of Highway 1 often. Our dinner was wonderful, and our server was especially personable and memorable. It felt as if we had been transported back in time to a location that had been there forever. Over the next three years, we would frequently return to Nick's Cove for lunch and dinner.

In 2010, when our son was in first grade, the father of one of his best friends worked as a manager at Nick's Cove. He told me that

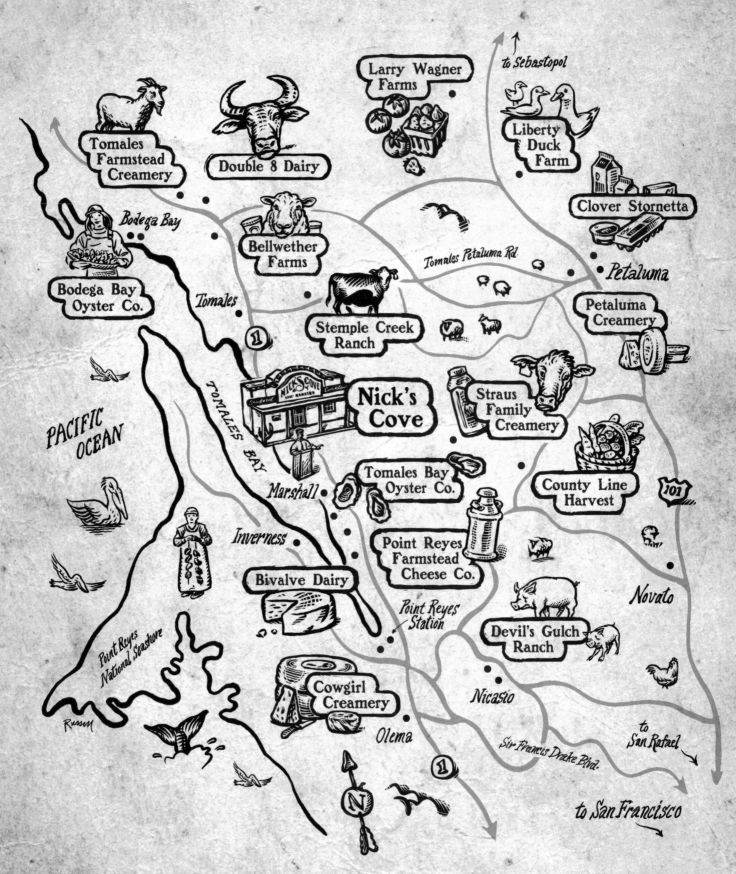

Tomales Farmstead Creamery

Double 8 Dairy

Larry Wagner Farms

to Sebastopol

Liberty Duck Farm

Clover Stornetta

Bodega Bay

Bodega Bay Oyster Co.

Bellwether Farms

Tomales Petaluma Rd.

Petaluma

Tomales

Stemple Creek Ranch

Petaluma Creamery

PACIFIC OCEAN

Nick's Cove

Straus Family Creamery

County Line Harvest

101

TOMALES BAY

Marshall

Tomales Bay Oyster Co.

Inverness

Point Reyes Farmstead Cheese Co.

Novato

Bivalve Dairy

Point Reyes Station

Devil's Gulch Ranch

Point Reyes National Seashore

Russell

Cowgirl Creamery

Nicasio

to San Rafael

Olema

Sir Francis Drake Blvd.

N

1

to San Francisco

the ownership group, headed up by Pat Kuleto, was looking to hire a part-time accounting and human resources director for that location. I immediately contacted Kuleto, and after meeting with him, I was hired on the spot. I began working at Nick's Cove on July 1, 2010.

In 2011, the property was sold to one of the original investors, and I was asked to stay on to run the entire operation, putting to work my years of experience in human resources, accounting, and hospitality. Not long after, the new owner and I joined forces to start Highway 1 Hospitality, a hospitality management company, and the rest is history.

From day one, Nick's Cove was the darling of our hospitality management company. The property is delicate, refined, temperamental, fiercely strong, exquisite, and difficult, but when you are here, you experience such joy that all of the challenges fade. It is less of a property and more of a relationship that I must actively work on every day—and I do just that, with delight.

Today, Nick's Cove has an award-winning restaurant and beverage program. We harvest a large percentage of the vegetables and herbs we use in our restaurant and bar from our thriving garden, which we call the Croft. We employ anywhere from thirty to fifty people, depending on the season, and our management team exudes positive energy that is felt from every angle of the operation: kitchen to cottages, grounds to boat shack.

We make donations to several local nonprofits to help in their fundraising efforts, the receipts of which go toward caring for the hungry, children, the elderly, and the environment. We

support the Petaluma Educational Foundation, the Boys & Girls Club, and Mentor Me, all in Petaluma, as well as schools in West Marin and beyond. Every Tuesday, we sponsor a Locals' Night, an evening with free live music and a prix fixe menu, so our local community members can come in and enjoy dinner with their neighbors.

As I write this introduction, it has been a decade since I became involved with Nick's Cove, and this cookbook has been a dream of mine since those early days. Although not every recipe found in these pages is currently on the menu at Nick's Cove, each one represents someone or something special: a certain chef, pastry chef, up-and-coming line cook, or bartender; a specific ingredient grown in our Croft; or a dish that I fell in love with the moment I tried it and that has become a tried-and-true staple of our menu. They are all here for you to experience! As one of the owners of this magnificent property, I wanted to capture its essence in a way that not only provides delicious and fun recipes to make at home, but also showcases the magic of Nick's Cove through my eyes. While this property as it currently exists would not have been possible without the input of millions of dollars, Nick's Cove is primarily a historical masterpiece, and I am honored to be its ambassador and its preservationist.

Through the stories, recipes, and photographs that follow, I hope you will take away a bit of how our history and the history of this corner of the world has shaped what Nick's Cove is today. I also hope that with this book in your kitchen, you will feel as if you have brought home a piece of the magic that is Nick's Cove.

West Marin is home to a wide variety of animals, wild and otherwise. These furry Highland cattle are some of our favorite neighbors.

THE HISTORY OF NICK'S COVE AND TOMALES BAY

The beautiful Tomales Bay area has served as a depot for travelers and for local fishermen and agriculture since the mid-nineteenth century. Nick's Cove is one of the last remaining historic settlements still catering to the tourist trade along this picturesque coastline.

The property on which Nick's Cove now sits was originally part of Rancho Nicasio, an 1835 Mexican land grant comprising tens of thousands of acres stretching from the Nicasio Valley to Tomales Bay. Although the Mexican governor had awarded this vast holding to the Coast Miwok, by 1850, the year California gained statehood, they had lost control of much of it through seizure by non-Indians. In 1852, the state's newly minted Public Land Commission formalized ownership of the rancho lands by a handful of men. Three years later, the Coast Miwok, aware that the 1848 Treaty of Guadalupe Hidalgo guaranteed the honoring of land grants, appealed to the commission to respect the grant's original provisions. Their claim was denied.

In 1850, engineer and lawyer Henry W. Halleck had purchased over thirty thousand acres of Rancho Nicasio, including the bayside patch that would become the future home of Nick's Cove. Unlike many large landowners, he saw his acquisition as a quiet hunting and fishing retreat, not a source of monetary profit, and built a weekend house along Halleck Creek, near present-day Nicasio. At the beginning of the Civil War, Halleck, who had to leave the area to oversee the Union armies at the request

of President Lincoln, asked his lawyer to sell off his land in small parcels. One of the buyers was Jeremiah Blake, a young Easterner who had settled in the Tomales Bay area in the early 1850s. In time, Blake began growing vegetables and grain and raising dairy cows, all of which yielded goods that were in demand by the growing population to the south. He also planted hundreds of blue gum and other trees, some of which were likely harvested for commercial firewood. Part of his land was on the bay, and he constructed a wharf there that would later become known as Blake's Landing, which today lies just a few miles south of Nick's Cove.

Other farmers and dairymen in the area were expanding their operations as well, and all of them needed an easier, quicker way to move their goods to market. That need began to be met in the early 1870s, when tracks for the North Pacific Coast Railroad were laid along the Tomales Bay shorefront. Formally opened in 1875, the railroad was soon transporting

OPPOSITE, CLOCKWISE FROM TOP LEFT: *1859 map of the northern portion of Rancho Nicasio; General Henry Halleck; Blake's Landing, circa 1969; Jeremiah Ladd Blake of Blake's Landing, Tomales Bay, CA.*

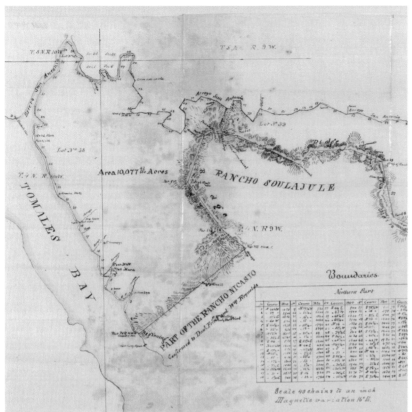

passengers, lumber, and local dairy and agricultural products along a continuous link between the Russian River area and Sausalito, where it connected to the ferry to San Francisco.

But it was the construction of State Route 1 in the early 1930s, followed by the opening of the Golden Gate Bridge in 1937, that brought a surge in tourists looking for food, lodging, and adventure. Marin County became a favorite destination for weekend motorists, and Tomales Bay was an especially popular choice because of its excellent fishing.

Others came to the area to put down roots. The similarity of Tomales Bay, with its mild winters and shallow waters, to the Adriatic coastline made it particularly appealing to people from that felicitous coastal stretch of Europe. Among them was the Nick Kojich family, who arrived in the area from Croatia in the late 1920s.

Nick and his wife Frances moved to the area to help Frances's brothers—Andy and Mike Matkovich—who owned and operated a local fishing business. Nick and Frances quickly fell in love with the location, the beauty of the

surrounding hillsides, and hiking in what is today the Point Reyes National Seashore, and founded what is now known as Nick's Cove.

In 1931, Nick and Frances Kojich purchased a parcel of the old Jeremiah Blake ranch, which is where Nick's Cove sits today. They moved several buildings and other structures from their Pierce Ranch property on the west side of Tomales Bay by barge. One of those original structures is what is now known as Bandit's Bungalow. They also moved an old herring-curing facility—the herring in Tomales Bay were once considered the best in the state—and set it up on pilings over the water. They renovated it and opened it as a small seafood restaurant selling shrimp and crab cocktails to passing

---

OPPOSITE, TOP: *Train traveling along Tomales Bay, circa 1914; train passengers would buy clams through the train windows from the little fishing settlement here, which was formerly called "Fisherman's" and is now called Marconi.* OPPOSITE, BOTTOM LEFT: *Oysters being harvested from Drakes Bay.* OPPOSITE, BOTTOM RIGHT: *Shell Beach, Tomales Bay (1950s).* BELOW, LEFT TO RIGHT: *Nick Kojich posing with his catch of the day in front of Nick's Cove; Andrew and Dorothy Matkovich; Andrew, Dorothy, Nick, and Judi (Andrew and Dorothy's daughter).*

tourists. With the end of Prohibition in 1933, Nick Kojich (a local bootlegger) began serving alcohol, too.

Many of the weekend travelers to Tomales Bay along the newly paved State Route 1 were fishermen and hunters, who knew that the bay waters and the sparsely settled countryside were rich in wildlife. Beginning in 1933, Nick and Frances were able to "capitalize" on this local appeal by renting out some of their waterfront cottages to these avid sportsmen from the San Francisco Bay Area, the Sacramento Valley, and beyond.

In 1950, shortly after a fire devastated the original building, Frances's nephew, Andrew Matkovich and his wife, Dorothy, bought into the business. Andrew felt quite at home at Nick's Cove—he had been born in Nick and Frances's home, which are now the cottages known as Fly Fisherman and Uncle Andy's. Andrew and his sisters attended Pierce School across the bay, and he grew up alongside his uncles, fishing and enjoying the peaceful surroundings of Tomales Bay.

In 1939, at the age of 21, Andrew and his father and sisters moved to Oakland. It was there that he met a beautiful young woman at a dance. Her name was Dorothy. In 1950, they

BELOW: *Nick's Cove, circa 1958.* OPPOSITE, CLOCKWISE FROM TOP LEFT: *Frances Kojich with Andrew and Dorothy Matkovich; Bob Brunner with his catch of the day; Dorothy Matkovich; participants from annual fishing derby, left to right—unknown, Milt Moyles, George Mallett, unknown, Nick Kojich on far right.*

began their next chapter with a move back to Andrew's childhood home of Marshall. After becoming partners in the business, Andrew quickly rebuilt the restaurant in the same location and reopened it with a full menu specializing in local seafood. Within a decade, Nick and Frances had retired and the Matkoviches were running the entire operation.

The Nick's Cove cabins continued to be a popular draw during the 1950s and 1960s as places where recreational fishermen could put up for the weekend or for long-term stays. Each year, the Matkovich family hosted fishing derbies for shark and stingray, as well as clam digs and crab feeds. Sportfishing was very popular in Tomales Bay at the time, and the two derbies were created to cut down on the "predators" that competed with the fishermen for the area's abundant silver salmon, steelhead, halibut, and flounder. Some visitors arrived by boat, which they would leave tied up at the pier while they went into the restaurant for a meal. Many commercial fishing boats also stopped to sell directly to the restaurant, a practice that determined the evening's menu. In the years that the Kojich and Matkovich families owned and operated Nick's Cove, they created an inviting, casual place that would become an institution attracting hunters, fishermen, nature lovers, and unsuspecting travelers who stumbled on a restaurant and bayside cottages full of character and surrounded by scenic beauty.

In 1973, the widowed Dorothy Matkovich sold Nick's Cove to Alfred and Ruth Gibson, ending more than sixty years of family ownership. During lunch with Ruth Gibson, she retold the story of how her first date with her future husband was actually a romantic drive out to Nick's Cove. That same day, Al told Ruth he had purchased the property and wanted her

help in running it! While they had never run a restaurant before, and had their own financial struggles through the years, they did their best to provide a place for travelers who wanted to escape the heat of the valley and enjoy a respite from their work in San Francisco. Over the years, guests included everyone from university professors, writers, and sportsmen to bird-watchers and kayakers.

After her husband's death, Ruth Gibson continued to operate the restaurant and cabin rentals until maintaining the property proved too costly.

In 1999, Ruth Gibson sold Nick's Cove to Pat Kuleto and Mark Franz, two prominent members of the Bay Area restaurant industry. Over the next seven years, the entire property underwent a major redevelopment that took great care to both maintain the integrity of its traditional architecture and reestablish its historical importance. Nick's Cove was reopened in July 2007 with a beautifully restored roadside bar, comfortable dining room, covered patio, rustic boat shack at the end of a four-hundred-foot-long pier, and twelve luxury cottages whose coastal vernacular style echoes the history of the community.

In 2011, the property changed hands again and to date remains a family-run operation and an iconic beacon surrounded by nature and offering the same warm hospitality that Nick and Frances Kojich established nearly ninety years ago.

PAGE 24, TOP: *Andrew Matkovich (left) with Nick Kojich (right) and patrons at the bar.* BOTTOM LEFT: *Andrew Matkovich shucking oysters behind the bar.* BOTTOM RIGHT: *Dorothy Kojich with Glen Nylander.* PAGE 25, TOP LEFT: *Al Gibson (right) with Anastacio Gonzales, known for his famous sauce.* TOP RIGHT: *Hand-painted sign for Nick's Cove, 1970s.* BOTTOM: *Ruth and Al Gibson.*

Starters

OYSTERS NICKERFELLER

⅔ cup plus 1 tablespoon unsalted butter, at room temperature

2 tablespoons minced shallot

1 teaspoon minced garlic

8 oz baby spinach

¼ cup anise-flavored liqueur (such as Pernod)

½ cup shredded semifirm cow's milk cheese (such as Toma or Gouda)

¼ cup chopped fresh tarragon

1 teaspoon kosher salt

24 small oysters, preferably Pacific Miyagi, each about 3 inches long

¼ cup fine dried bread crumbs (optional)

Makes 24 oysters; 4 to 6 servings

This recipe is Nick's Cove's take on oysters Rockefeller, a classic dish of gently baked oysters topped with buttery greens invented in 1889 at Antoine's, a famed New Orleans restaurant. It reportedly came about as a result of a shortage of French snails, which chef Jules Alciatore imaginatively replaced with oysters, a local shellfish available in abundance. He named the rich dish after John D. Rockefeller, who was the wealthiest American at the time, and gave it a topping the color of greenbacks. In our grilled version, we mix a local cheese, Toma, from the nearby Point Reyes Farmstead Cheese Company, with the spinach, as we like how it softens the flavor of the sometimes bitter green. If you cannot find Toma, any buttery, semifirm cow's milk cheese, such as Gouda, can be substituted.

In a skillet, melt 1 tablespoon of the butter over medium heat. Add the shallot and garlic and cook, stirring, until soft and translucent, about 5 minutes. Add the spinach and cook, stirring occasionally, until wilted, about 4 minutes longer. Pour in the liqueur and deglaze the pan, stirring to dislodge any browned bits from the pan bottom. Raise the heat to high and bring the mixture to a boil, then cook, stirring, until reduced by one-fourth, about 2 minutes.

Remove from the heat and let cool slightly, then transfer to a food processor and pulse until smooth. Add the remaining ⅔ cup butter, the cheese, tarragon, and salt and pulse until the ingredients are well combined. Set aside.

Rinse the oysters under cold running water and scrub clean with a stiff brush. To shuck each oyster, hold the oyster, flat side up, on a folded kitchen towel in your nondominant hand. Find the small opening between the shells in the pointed, hinged end, insert the tip of an oyster knife into the gap, and twist the tip until the hinge pops. Slide the knife in between the shells and run the blade along the top shell to cut the muscle that attaches the oyster to it. Then carefully run the blade along the bottom shell, freeing the oyster from it. Lift off and discard the top shell, keeping the oyster and juices in the bottom shell. Set aside on a sheet pan. Repeat with the remaining oysters.

Prepare a charcoal or gas grill for direct cooking over high heat (450°F). Brush the grill grate clean.

Top each oyster with about 2 teaspoons of the butter-spinach mixture. Arrange the oysters on the grill, close the cover, and grill until the butter melts and the juices start to bubble, 2 to 4 minutes. Using tongs, transfer the oysters to a serving platter. Garnish with the bread crumbs, if using. Serve at once.

OYSTERS MORNAY

For the Mornay sauce:
4 tablespoons unsalted butter
¼ cup all-purpose flour
1 cup whole milk
1 cup heavy cream
¼ cup shredded Gruyère cheese
¼ cup shredded white Cheddar
  cheese
2 tablespoons grated Parmesan
  cheese
Pinch of freshly grated nutmeg
Juice of ½ lemon
Kosher salt

24 small oysters, preferably Pacific
  Miyagi, each about 3 inches long
¼ cup fine dried bread crumbs
¼ cup grated Parmesan cheese

Makes 24 oysters; 4 to 6 servings

Commonly referred to as the "gateway dish to oysters" by the Nick's Cove staff, this version is indeed a great introduction to cooked oysters. Topped with Mornay sauce—the classic French cheese sauce—and crunchy bread crumbs, what's not to like? That combination might make some wonder if the oyster is even necessary, but my answer is always "Absolutely!" As with all our grilled oyster dishes, choose oysters about 3 inches long. If they are smaller, they can too easily overcook. If they are too big, they are more than a mouthful!

To make the sauce, in a heavy medium saucepan, melt the butter over medium heat. Add the flour and whisk until smooth, then cook, stirring constantly, until the mixture bubbles and smells of shortbread, about 1 minute. While whisking constantly, slowly add the milk, continuing to whisk until the mixture is smooth. Cook, whisking often, until the mixture boils gently and thickens, about 7 minutes.

Reduce the heat to low and pour in the cream while whisking constantly. Return the sauce to a simmer; add the Gruyère, Cheddar, and Parmesan, and whisk until the cheese has melted and the sauce is smooth. Stir in the nutmeg and lemon juice and season to taste with salt. Remove from the heat and cover to keep warm.

Rinse the oysters under cold running water and scrub clean with a stiff brush. To shuck each oyster, hold the oyster, flat side up, on a folded kitchen towel in your nondominant hand. Find the small opening between the shells in the pointed, hinged end, insert the tip of an oyster knife into the gap, and then twist the tip until the hinge pops. Slide the knife in between the shells and run the blade along the top shell to cut the muscle that attaches the oyster to it. Then carefully run the blade along the bottom shell, freeing the oyster from it. Lift off and discard the top shell, keeping the oyster and juices in the bottom shell. Set aside on a sheet pan. Repeat with the remaining oysters.

Prepare a charcoal or gas grill for direct cooking over high heat (450°F). Brush the grill grate clean.

Top each oyster with about 1 tablespoon of the sauce. Arrange the oysters on the grill, close the cover, and grill until the juices start to bubble, 2 to 4 minutes. Using tongs, transfer the oysters to a serving plate. Garnish with the bread crumbs and Parmesan. Serve at once.

TOMALES BAY OYSTERS

West Marin is rich in oyster culture: growing, harvesting, shucking, and devouring. And a Nick's Cove cookbook would not be complete without talking about these ubiquitous and tasty bivalves.

A number of oyster farms lie to the north and south of Nick's Cove on Tomales Bay, including Hog Island Oyster Company, Tomales Bay Oyster Company (referred to locally as TBOC), and Bodega Bay Oyster Company, as well as operations by smaller farmers who rent space from some of the larger producers. These local businesses

launch their boats at Miller Boat Launch, adjacent to Nick's Cove, and are busy pulling in the daily harvest as many of our guests are waking up for the day and members of our staff are arriving to begin theirs.

Throughout the week, droves of cars make their way along serpentine Highway 1. Many stop along this eastern stretch of the highway for the devouring part of West Marin's oyster culture. From folks shucking their own on bayside tables at our neighbors to the south to guests enjoying them on the half shell while sipping hand-crafted cocktails at our own celebrated roadside bar, the town of Marshall is known worldwide for its oyster scene. Although we do not farm oysters like many of our nearby friends, we most certainly sell a lot of them, and we are proud to support the oyster farmers of Tomales Bay.

THAI GREEN CURRY OYSTERS

½ cup coconut milk

Leafy tops from 2 bunches cilantro

6 green onions, white and green parts, roughly chopped

2 tablespoons peeled and grated fresh ginger

2 cloves garlic, roughly chopped

½ jalapeño chile, seeded and roughly chopped

1 lemongrass stalk, bulb portion only, root end trimmed, tough outer leaves discarded, and thinly sliced crosswise

1 tablespoon Asian fish sauce

Juice of 1 lime

24 small oysters, preferably Pacific Miyagi, each about 3 inches long

½ cup unsalted roasted peanuts, crushed

Makes 24 oysters; 4 to 6 servings

Citrusy lemongrass, bright-tasting cilantro, fiery chile, and spicy ginger flavor these Southeast Asian–inspired grilled oysters by chef Kua Speer. The coconut milk tones down the heat of the jalapeño and helps all of the flavors to blend—a mix that complements the brininess of the oysters. Be sure to use only the yellow bulb-like portion of the lemongrass, discarding the grassy tops and root end and peeling away the fibrous leaves until you reach the tender center.

In a blender, combine the coconut milk, cilantro, green onions, ginger, garlic, chile, lemongrass, fish sauce, and lime juice and blend on high speed until the mixture is almost smooth, about 1 minute. Transfer to a small bowl.

Rinse the oysters under cold running water and scrub clean with a stiff brush. To shuck each oyster, hold the oyster, flat side up, on a folded kitchen towel in your nondominant hand. Find the small opening between the shells in the pointed, hinged end, insert the tip of an oyster knife into the gap, and then twist the tip until the hinge pops. Slide the knife between the shells and run the blade along the top shell to cut the muscle that attaches the oyster to it. Then carefully run the blade along the bottom shell, freeing the oyster from it. Lift off and discard the top shell, keeping the oyster and juices in the bottom shell. Set aside on a sheet pan. Repeat with the remaining oysters.

Prepare a charcoal or gas grill for direct cooking over high heat (450°F). Brush the grill grate clean.

Top each oyster with about 1½ tablespoons of the green curry mixture. Arrange the oysters on the grill, close the cover, and grill until the juices start to bubble, 2 to 4 minutes. Using tongs, transfer the oysters to a serving plate. Garnish with the peanuts and serve right away.

VERSATILITY TIP

This versatile curry sauce is great to have in your repertoire. Brush it on shrimp or chicken while grilling, or use it as a sauce for pan-seared flaky white fish or sautéed veggies and rice. If using as a sauce, simmer the sauce gently for 2 or 3 minutes in a pan over medium-low heat before using.

HEIRLOOM TOMATO-HERB BRUSCHETTA
WITH BALSAMIC GLAZE

For the balsamic glaze:
½ cup balsamic vinegar
2 tablespoons sugar
½ teaspoon kosher salt
1 bay leaf

For the tomato-herb topping:
2 heirloom tomatoes, cut into
 ½-inch cubes
10 fresh basil leaves, thinly sliced
1 large clove garlic, minced
2 teaspoons minced fresh
 oregano leaves
2 tablespoons extra-virgin olive oil
½ teaspoon kosher salt

8 slices baguette, cut on the diagonal,
 each about 4 inches long and
 ½ inch thick
¼ cup extra-virgin olive oil

Makes 4 servings

Sonoma County farmer Larry Wagner grows award-winning tomatoes, and we are lucky enough to be among only a handful of local restaurants that receive his beauties throughout the summer. When the season is over for Larry's plants, we extend our bounty with vine-ripened tomatoes from our Croft. Its microclimate, along with help from the large grove of cypress trees across the road, provides just the right spot for tomatoes to thrive into the fall. To showcase the simple perfection of sun-ripened tomatoes, we serve them on toasted bread with a balsamic glaze and some fresh herbs. A creamy local burrata would be a great addition to this dish.

Preheat the oven to 350°F.

To make the glaze, in a small saucepan, combine the vinegar, sugar, salt, and bay leaf and bring to a simmer over medium-high heat, stirring to dissolve the sugar and salt. Continue to simmer, stirring occasionally, until syrupy and reduced by about half, about 8 minutes. Remove from the heat, discard the bay leaf, and let cool to room temperature.

While the glaze cools, make the topping. In a medium bowl, combine the tomatoes, basil, garlic, oregano, oil, and salt and stir to mix well.

Brush both sides of each baguette slice with the oil and arrange on a large sheet pan. Toast in the oven, turning once, until lightly browned, about 10 minutes.

Transfer the toasted baguette slices to a large platter or cutting board. Top each slice with about 2 tablespoons of the tomato mixture and then drizzle with the glaze. Serve at once.

Fun Fact

Bruschetta originated in Italy in the fifteenth century as a way of salvaging bread that had gone stale. Legend has it that the first bruschetta came from Tuscan tomato farmers and laborers who would rub day-old pieces of bread with fresh ripe tomatoes as a snack.

NICK'S COVE CHEESE BOARD

Choose three or four cheeses for your board. Here are some of my favorites:

Point Reyes Farmstead Cheese
  Company (cow)
Double 8 Dairy (water buffalo/cow)
Toluma Farms & Tomales
  Farmstead Creamery (goat/sheep)
Cowgirl Creamery (cow)
Laura Chenel (goat)
Bellwether Farms (cow/sheep)
Marin French Cheese (cow)
Nicasio Valley Cheese (cow)
Petaluma Creamery (cow)
Achadinha Cheese (goat)
Valley Ford Cheese
  & Creamery (cow)

Choose as many accents as you like:

Toasted nuts
Olives
Fruit, such as figs or sliced apples
Jam, marmalade, chutney, or other
  preserves or fruit pastes

Choose crackers and/or bread:

Sliced baguette
Plain or seeded crackers

Marin and Sonoma Counties are home to some of the most amazing cheesemakers in the country, so the hardest part of putting together one of our cheese boards is limiting it to only a few of the options available to us. In order to support our local cheesemakers—our neighbors—we rotate our choices every couple of months. Some of my favorites include cow's milk cheeses from Point Reyes Farmstead Cheese Company, goat's and sheep's milk cheeses from Toluma Farms & Tomales Farmstead Creamery, and buffalo's milk mozzarella from Double 8 Dairy. The cheeses listed are just a sampling of the many different cheesemakers located near Nick's Cove and represent what might be found on our menu on any given day. If you like, expand your cheese board with a selection of charcuterie.

Offer at least three different types of cheese according to aging, including soft, semifirm, and hard. To enhance the selection, provide a mix of major milk types—cow, goat, sheep—and of styles beyond aging, such as blue or washed rind. Allow 2 to 3 ounces of cheese per guest and be sure to remove hard and semifirm cheeses from the refrigerator about an hour before they will be served so they will come to room temperature.

Then, choose as many accents as you like. I like something salty, like nuts and olives. Fresh fruit helps balance the richness of the cheese with sweetness and acid (I suggest figs when in season or sliced apples for their crisp texture). And jam, marmalade, chutney, or a fruit paste also balance well with cheese. I recommend persimmon preserves.

Finally, choose crackers and/or bread. With so many options, it is easy to get overwhelmed by the choices. I prefer to keep the selection simple so the cheese stands out, rather than being overpowered by a strong, heavily flavored cracker or bread. Offer plain or seeded crackers, and you can never go wrong with a thinly sliced sourdough baguette.

Put it all together: Choose a large board or a flat platter. Set out the soft and semi-soft cheeses whole with a knife nearby, and preslice about half of any firm cheese you serve. Also preslice the fruits so they are easy to pick up and graze on, and offer bowls of olives, toasted or even candied nuts for a little extra sweetness, and a preserve or two.

Now that you have the guidelines on what and how much to have on your board, let your board be a reflection of your entertaining style. Get creative, have fun, and make it interesting! For each cheese, I like to create a label, including the cheesemaker's name, the name of the cheese, and the type of milk it is made from so my friends know more about what they are enjoying.

Local Cheesemakers

By the mid-1800s, Marin and Sonoma Counties were dotted with small, family-operated dairy farms and were well known for the high quality of their milk (see page 136). Today, many dairy farms remain, and while some farmers still produce milk for bottling, several others have turned to making award-winning cheeses from the milk produced on their farm and/or purchased from neighboring dairies. These amazing local cheesemakers are making everything from aged mixed-milk cheeses to fresh buffalo mozzarella and everything in between.

The products of many of our local cheesemakers, such as Point Reyes Farmstead Cheese, Toluma Farms & Tomales Farmstead Creamery, Nicasio Valley Cheese Company, Cowgirl Creamery, Valley Ford Cheese & Creamery, and more, can be found on our menu as an ingredient in our dishes, such as our popular Dungeness Crab Mac and Cheese (page 90), or featured on our cheese boards. Many of these same artisanal cheesemakers welcome visitors to the region for tours and/or tastings of their cheese. This steadily growing agritourism now taking shape along Highway 1 and beyond makes this a thrilling time to be in business in West Marin.

Gambonini Dairy on Petaluma Marshall Road, Tomales, CA, with Gambonini family members, employees, and their cows in front of the main barn; 1898.

DUNGENESS CRAB CAKES

WITH SPICY PAPRIKA MAYO

For the spicy paprika mayo:
¾ cup mayonnaise
2 tablespoons smoked paprika
3 tablespoons fresh lemon juice
¼ teaspoon cayenne pepper,
   or to taste
Kosher salt

For the crab cakes:
1 lb fresh-cooked Dungeness
   crabmeat, picked over for
   shell fragments
1 cup mayonnaise
2¼ cups panko (Japanese
   bread crumbs)
1 tablespoon Old Bay seasoning
2 teaspoons smoked paprika
1 teaspoon kosher salt

½ cup canola oil
1 lemon, cut into 6 wedges

Makes 6 servings

Panfried until crispy and golden brown, our crab cakes are hearty and rich, packed full of the local Dungeness crab, coated with just a thin layer of bread crumbs to hold everything together, and drizzled with a paprika-spiced mayonnaise. A simple salad of arugula, shaved fennel, and chives dressed with Champagne vinaigrette is a nice accompaniment. Of course, a glass of bubbly would also be a welcome pairing.

To make the mayo, in a small bowl, whisk together the mayonnaise, paprika, lemon juice, and cayenne, mixing well. Taste and adjust the seasoning with salt and cayenne if needed. Cover and refrigerate until ready to serve. (The mayo can be made up to 4 days in advance.)

To make the crab cakes, in a medium bowl, combine the crabmeat, mayonnaise, ¼ cup of the panko, the Old Bay seasoning, paprika, and salt. Using your hands, gently mix together the ingredients, breaking up any large lumps of crabmeat and feeling for any errant bits of shell that may remain. Divide the mixture into six equal portions, each about ¼ cup. Shape each portion into a cake and set aside on a sheet pan. Pour the remaining 2 cups panko into a wide, shallow bowl. One at a time, press each crab cake into the panko, coating evenly on all sides.

Preheat the oven to 200°F. Line a second sheet pan with paper towels. In a large skillet, warm the oil over medium-high heat. When the oil is hot, working in batches if necessary to avoid crowding, arrange the cakes in the pan, spacing them about ½ inch apart. Cook, turning once, until golden brown on both sides, about 6 minutes total. Using a slotted spatula, transfer to the towel-lined pan to drain and place in the oven to keep warm. Repeat with the remaining cakes.

Serve the crab cakes warm, drizzled with the mayo, with a wedge of lemon on the side.

DID YOU KNOW?

The first published crab cake recipe originated in Baltimore in 1930, using blue crabs. Out here on the West Coast, we are partial to our local, buttery Dungeness crab, but you can use any fresh, local crab that you prefer. We highly recommend not using canned crabmeat, as the flavor of the cakes depends on the highest-quality, freshest crab you can find.

Fishing boat across from Marshall Beach on the southwest side of Tomales Bay.

AHI TUNA POKE

WITH PICKLED VEGETABLES

For the pickled vegetables:

1½ cups unseasoned rice vinegar

1 tablespoon peeled and minced fresh ginger

1 tablespoon kosher salt

1 tablespoon sugar

½ cup ice cubes (about 4 large cubes)

3 small radishes, such as Easter Egg radishes, trimmed and thinly sliced

1 small Japanese or English cucumber, very thinly sliced (about 1/16 inch thick)

For the poke:

1 cup low-sodium soy sauce

1 tablespoon toasted sesame oil

¼ cup thinly sliced red onion

2 teaspoons peeled and minced fresh ginger

2 teaspoons minced fresh garlic

2 teaspoons Sriracha sauce or wasabi paste (optional)

2 teaspoons white sesame seeds

2 lb sashimi-grade ahi (yellowtail) tuna, cut into ½-inch cubes

2 green onions, green parts only, thinly sliced

Makes 4 to 6 servings

Chef Kua Speer grew up in Hawaii, so he knows his way around tuna poke. This version is light and delicate, and we like serving it with pickled vegetables rather than crackers for a tangy twist. Be sure to use a non-vinegar-based hot sauce and to pickle the vegetables a day in advance to allow time for them to soak up all the good vinegary flavor. If the blood line (deep red, blood-rich muscle) has not been removed from the tuna, trim it away before cutting up the fish, as it has a strong, fishy flavor.

To make the pickled vegetables, in a small saucepan, combine the vinegar, ginger, salt, and sugar and bring to a simmer over medium heat, stirring to dissolve the salt and sugar. Remove from the heat and set aside for 15 minutes.

Put the ice into a medium bowl. Strain the vinegar mixture through a fine-mesh sieve into the bowl of ice. Divide the cold pickling liquid evenly between two small bowls, then add the radishes to one bowl and the cucumber to the second bowl. Cover the bowls tightly with plastic wrap and refrigerate for at least 24 hours or up to 5 days.

To make the poke, in a small bowl, whisk together the soy sauce, sesame oil, red onion, ginger, garlic, and Sriracha (if using) until well combined. Cover and set aside for 1 hour at room temperature or refrigerate for up to 1 day.

In a small dry skillet, toast the sesame seeds over medium heat, stirring often, until lightly golden, about 2 minutes. Pour onto a small plate and let cool.

Put the tuna into a medium bowl. Strain the soy sauce mixture through the fine-mesh sieve over the tuna, then toss to coat evenly. Add the sesame seeds and green onions to the tuna and stir to mix.

Pile the tuna mixture onto a serving plate. Remove the radish and cucumber slices from the pickling liquid and arrange around the poke mixture. Serve at once.

Hog Island

Located across from Nick's Cove in Tomales Bay, and owned by the Point Reyes National Seashore, Hog Island is currently an uninhabited bird sanctuary and pupping ground for harbor seals. According to legend, in the late nineteenth century, a barge carrying pigs caught fire, ran aground on the island to prevent sinking, and all the pigs promptly ran off. Although the escapees were eventually rounded up, the name Hog Island stuck. Its smaller sister island, commonly referred to as either Duck Island or Piglet, is connected by a narrow shoal only rarely visible during low tide.

Although Hog Island is now off-limits to the public to preserve the wildlife habitat and prevent further erosion, you can still see the ruins of a small structure, evidence that at one time someone likely lived there.

This two-acre island is very close to my heart. In June 1996, after a beautiful day of kayaking in Tomales Bay, my boyfriend pulled our boat up to the shore of the island and, on bended knee, proposed to me. I said, "Yes!" and we were married a year later.

Hog Island, circa 2015.

SHRIMP COCKTAIL
WITH TOMATILLO AND AVOCADO

For the shrimp:

½ small white onion, roughly
  chopped

1 celery stalk, roughly chopped

1 clove garlic, roughly chopped

1 lemon, halved

2 bay leaves

2 tablespoons kosher salt

1 tablespoon black peppercorns

1 lb large shrimp in the shell, peeled
  and deveined

For the tomatillo salsa:

8 tomatillos, papery husks removed,
  rinsed, and quartered

1 small jalapeño chile, halved
  lengthwise and seeded

2 cloves garlic

1 teaspoon kosher salt

Juice of 5 limes (about ½ cup)

Leaves from ½ bunch cilantro,
  chopped

½ small red onion, minced

2 avocados, halved, pitted, peeled,
  and cut into ¼-inch pieces

3 limes, quartered

1 (14-oz) bag tortilla chips

Makes 4 to 6 servings

In this California riff on the classic shrimp cocktail, tomatillo salsa delivers bright acidity while avocado provides creaminess. If possible, make the tomatillo salsa the night before serving so the flavors have time to meld. You can also combine the shrimp and the salsa up to a day in advance of serving. **We have not completely dispensed with tradition, however. We often offer a classic shrimp cocktail—shrimp with a tangy, tomatoey cocktail sauce—on our kids' menu, where it is regularly ordered by adults.**

To poach the shrimp, fill a large bowl half full with water and ice. In a large pot, combine the white onion, celery, garlic, lemon, bay leaves, salt, peppercorns, and 3 qt water and bring to a boil over high heat, stirring to dissolve the salt. Add the shrimp, adjust the heat to maintain a simmer, and cook the shrimp until they turn pink and are opaque and cooked through, about 6 minutes. Using a slotted spoon, transfer the shrimp to the ice bath. Once they are cool, drain them, pat dry, and cut into ½-inch pieces. Transfer to a large airtight container and refrigerate until ready to use.

To make the tomatillo salsa, in a large saucepan, combine the tomatillos, chile, garlic, salt, and 6 cups water and bring to a boil over high heat. Reduce the heat to medium and simmer until the tomatillos soften, about 20 minutes.

Remove from the heat and drain through a sieve placed over a bowl. Let the solids and the cooking liquid cool slightly, then transfer the solids and 1 cup of the liquid to a blender. Add the lime juice and blend on medium speed to a smooth puree. Transfer to a medium bowl and let cool to room temperature.

Add the tomatillo salsa, cilantro, and red onion to the container of shrimp. Stir to mix well, then cover and refrigerate for at least 2 hours or up to overnight.

To assemble the dish, transfer the shrimp mixture to a wide, shallow serving bowl and top with the avocado in an even layer. Arrange the lime quarters around the edge of the bowl. Serve with the tortilla chips alongside for scooping up the shrimp-tomatillo cocktail.

WILD ARUGULA CAKES

For the arugula cakes:
3 lb arugula, roughly chopped
1½ cups panko (Japanese bread
    crumbs)
¾ cup fromage blanc or
    mascarpone cheese
¼ cup grated Parmesan cheese
2 large eggs, lightly beaten
2 shallots, minced
1 clove garlic, minced
Pinch of freshly grated nutmeg
1 tablespoon kosher salt

For coating:
2 cups all-purpose flour
4 large eggs, lightly beaten
3 cups panko

Canola or peanut oil, for frying

Makes 12 cakes; 6 servings

For a while, we had an abundance of wild arugula growing in our Croft. At lunch one day, our chef at the time, Austin Perkins, presented me with two perfectly golden brown, crispy cakes made from that arugula. I cut into one of them and the most brilliant green leaves greeted me. I took a bite and swooned. The cakes can be cut to any size and are great as a side to fish or quail. They would also make a delicious vegetarian main course if served alongside a bowl of roasted red pepper and tomato soup. We use local cheesemaker Bellwether Farms' fromage blanc, a light, silky European-style fresh cheese that is easy to spread. It's a bit salty and tart, and any leftover cheese is delicious spread on a toasted bagel for breakfast. Instead of arugula, you can substitute the same amount of baby spinach, chard, or mustard greens, all of which will be slightly less peppery than arugula.

To make the cakes, fill a large saucepan two-thirds full with salted water and bring to a boil over high heat. Add the arugula and blanch, stirring, for 1 minute. Drain into a fine-mesh sieve, then run under cold running water to stop the cooking. Using your hands, squeeze as much water as possible out of the greens. Transfer to a large bowl.

Add the panko, fromage blanc, Parmesan, eggs, shallots, garlic, nutmeg, and salt to the greens and stir to mix well. Spread the mixture evenly on a 9-by-13-inch sheet pan. Transfer to the freezer to freeze slightly, 40 to 60 minutes.

Cut the arugula mixture into twelve 3-inch squares. Have ready a large platter. To assemble the coating, line up three shallow, small bowls. Put the flour into one bowl, crack the eggs into a second bowl and beat until blended, and put the panko into the third bowl. One at a time, dredge the arugula cakes evenly in the flour, tapping off the excess; then coat both sides in the egg, allowing the excess to drip off; and finally, coat evenly with the panko, pressing them to adhere. As each cake is ready, set it aside on the platter.

Line a second large platter with paper towels and set it near the stove. Pour the oil to a depth of 2 inches into a large, deep, heavy saucepan or pot and heat over medium heat to 350°F on a deep-fry thermometer. Working in batches of about four cakes at a time, carefully add the cakes to the hot oil and fry, turning once or twice with tongs, until crispy and golden brown, about 1 minute. Using the tongs, transfer to the towel-lined plate to drain. Serve hot.

HAND-CUT KENNEBEC FRIES

3 lb Kennebec potatoes (see
Chef's Tip), peeled
Canola oil, for deep-frying
Kosher salt

Makes 4 to 6 servings

If you walk by the kitchen in the early morning, you just might hear the "thump, thump, thump" of the kitchen staff running potatoes through the cutter by hand to make our sought-after fries. Extra crispy on the outside and blissfully creamy inside, our fries are our most ordered side dish. They are so good because we use Kennebec potatoes, which have thin, pale tan skin; a high-starch, low-moisture white flesh; and a distinctive nutty flavor. Then we fry them not once but twice. Most Kennebecs go to big commercial operations for making chips, so they can be difficult to find at retail groceries. But it is worth it to ask the produce manager at your local market about their availability. In keeping with our coastal vibe, I like my heap of fries with the salty goodness of a little *furikake* sprinkled on top. Truffle fries are also a Nick's Cove favorite.

Cut the potatoes lengthwise into ¼-inch-thick slices. Stack the slices and cut the stack lengthwise into sticks ¼ inch wide and thick. Fill a large Dutch oven or other heavy pot half full with oil. Place over high heat and heat until the oil registers 325°F on a deep-fry thermometer. Set one or more cooling racks on a large sheet pan and line the rack(s) with paper towels. Place the setup near the stove.

When the oil is ready, working in batches of about 1 cup, carefully add the potatoes to the hot oil and fry them, turning them as they cook with a heatproof slotted spoon, for 2 minutes. They will still be pale and about half-cooked and should bend but not snap. Using the spoon, transfer the fries to the towel-lined rack. Repeat with the remaining potatoes. Let the fries cool to room temperature.

Preheat the oven to 200°F. When the fries have cooled, reheat the oil to 350°F on the thermometer. Working again in batches of about 1 cup, fry the potatoes, stirring with the slotted spoon, until golden brown, about 3 minutes. Using the slotted spoon, transfer the fries to a large, wide heatproof bowl and toss with a little salt. Transfer the bowl to the oven to keep warm while you repeat to cook and season all of the remaining fries. Serve at once.

CHEF'S TIP

If you cannot find Kennebecs, russet potatoes are a good substitute, but you must start the recipe a day in advance. Peel and cut the russets as directed, rinse under cold water, and soak in a large bowl filled with cold water in the refrigerator overnight. The next day, drain the potatoes, pat them dry with paper towels, and then fry them twice as directed.

KALE, PANCETTA, TOMATO, AND FETA SALAD

WITH BALSAMIC VINAIGRETTE

For the balsamic vinaigrette:
¼ cup white or red balsamic vinegar
1 small shallot, minced
1 teaspoon Dijon mustard
½ cup extra-virgin olive oil
Kosher salt and freshly ground
  black pepper

8 oz pancetta, cut into ¼-inch pieces
2 bunches kale (such as Red Russian),
  tough stems and ribs removed and
  leaves cut into ½-inch-wide strips
1 pt cherry tomatoes, quartered
  lengthwise
½ cup crumbled feta cheese

Makes 6 servings

This simple salad is a great way to showcase the wealth of kale from our on-site garden. The more you massage the kale, the softer the leaves become and the more enjoyable the salad is to eat. We always try to use homegrown tomatoes and a local feta, such as Kota'lo from Tomales Farmstead Creamery. Transform this salad into a main course by topping it with grilled chicken or salmon.

To make the vinaigrette, in a small bowl, whisk together the vinegar, shallot, and mustard. Slowly add the oil in a thin stream while whisking vigorously until emulsified. Season to taste with salt and pepper. (The vinaigrette will keep in an airtight container in the refrigerator for up to 1 week.)

Line a plate with paper towels and set it near the stove. In a medium skillet, cook the pancetta over medium heat, stirring occasionally, until it starts to render its fat and become crisp, about 10 minutes. Using a slotted spoon, transfer to the towel-lined plate to drain.

In a large bowl, drizzle the kale with ½ cup of the dressing. Using your hands, gently massage the kale until it softens, about 2 minutes. If you would like to add more dressing, do so now and toss to coat. Add the pancetta, tomatoes, and feta and toss gently to mix evenly. Serve at once.

SEASONALITY

There is really no substitute for ripe cherry tomatoes, picked fresh at the height of summer. If tomatoes are not in season, we suggest substituting roasted cubed butternut squash, asparagus, or charred broccoli florets.

LITTLE GEM LETTUCES

WITH RADISHES AND HERB BUTTERMILK DRESSING

For the herb buttermilk dressing:
1 cup buttermilk
¼ cup loosely packed chopped
  green onions, green parts only
¼ cup loosely packed chopped
  fresh flat-leaf parsley leaves
¼ cup loosely packed chopped
  fresh basil leaves
2 tablespoons firmly packed
  chopped fresh tarragon leaves
1 tablespoon firmly packed chopped
  fresh sage leaves
1 tablespoon mayonnaise
2 teaspoons Dijon mustard
½ teaspoon kosher salt
¼ cup extra-virgin olive oil

For the croutons:
½ baguette (about 6 oz), hand-torn
  into 1-inch pieces
¼ cup extra-virgin olive oil
1 tablespoon minced garlic

For the salad:
3 heads Little Gem lettuce
5 French Breakfast or Easter Egg
  radishes, trimmed and sliced
  paper-thin

Makes 6 servings

The beautiful lettuces and radishes we use in this popular salad are grown in our Croft. We let the lettuce shine by cutting the tender heads in half lengthwise. That way you can see the stunning color inside. The buttermilk dressing makes great use of our bountiful kitchen herb garden. But be forewarned: the dressing is so delectable you will want to put it on everything.

To make the dressing, in a blender, combine the buttermilk, green onions, parsley, basil, tarragon, sage, mayonnaise, mustard, and salt and blend on medium-high speed until smooth. Transfer to a medium bowl and slowly add the oil while whisking constantly until the mixture emulsifies. Taste and adjust the seasoning with salt. Cover and refrigerate for at least 3 hours before using. (The dressing will keep in an airtight container in the refrigerator for up to 5 days.)

To make the croutons, preheat the oven to 350°F. In a large bowl, toss the bread pieces with the oil and garlic, coating evenly. Pour onto a sheet pan, spread into a single layer, and bake, stirring once halfway through baking, until golden brown, about 14 minutes.

To assemble the salads, halve each lettuce head lengthwise, then carefully cut away most of the core, leaving enough intact to keep the leaves attached. Place a lettuce half, cut side up, on each of six individual plates. Sprinkle half of the radish slices over the salads, dividing them evenly, and then drizzle each salad with ¼ cup of the dressing, starting at the top of the head and continuing to the base. Divide the croutons evenly among the salads, then sprinkle the salads with the remaining radishes, again dividing them evenly. Serve at once.

HEALTHY TIP

We love using buttermilk whenever possible because it is not only tangy and delicious, but it's high in probiotics and protein and low in fat. If you can get fresh, cultured buttermilk from a local producer there is nothing like it!

THE CROFT

One day in 2011, I drove to Yountville to tour the gardens of the famed French Laundry and was quickly enamored with the stunning beds of perfectly tended vegetables that were being grown for the restaurant kitchen. From that moment, I was on a quest to create a version of that garden at Nick's Cove.

Although we had terraced areas from which to start, our beds were overrun with weeds, and it took months just to get to the dirt. And when we did, we found that it was hard, undernourished, rocky soil. That first year, the team worked tirelessly to prepare the terraces for planting. The following year, we had our first harvest!

I was so proud of how the garden was coming together. I wanted it to have its own identity and to celebrate its significance to the restaurant. I wanted something closer than farm-to-table. One day my marketing assistant said, "I found the perfect name: let's call it the Croft." A croft is defined as "a small plot of ground adjacent to a house and used as a kitchen garden large enough to feed a family or have commercial value." While the

definition does not exactly match what we have, I loved the name immediately.

The Croft has been in full production for the past seven seasons. Our farming team harvests some of the most delectable fruits and vegetables from it: tomatoes, tomatillos, lettuces, beans, cucumbers, chard, broccoli, radishes, melons, asparagus—the list goes on. While not certified organic, our vegetables, flowers, and herbs are grown with regenerative and organic practices to ensure our soil is healthy for years to come so that we can continue to sustain our kitchen garden for generations.

WARM ROASTED CAULIFLOWER SALAD

WITH PANCETTA AND MUSTARD VINAIGRETTE

For the cauliflower:
1 head cauliflower, cored and cut
into 1-inch florets
3 tablespoons extra-virgin olive oil
Kosher salt and freshly ground
black pepper

For the mustard vinaigrette:
1 shallot, minced
¼ cup whole-grain mustard
3 tablespoons Champagne vinegar
¼ cup extra-virgin olive oil

2 tablespoons extra-virgin olive oil
6 oz pancetta, cut into ¼-inch cubes
8 oz arugula

Makes 2 to 4 servings

This tangy, whole-grain mustard vinaigrette imbues cauliflower with deep flavor. Salty pancetta and peppery arugula are natural partners and help make this salad anything but ordinary. The vinaigrette would also be good on any of your favorite roasted or grilled vegetables. This salad is excellent as a side to any grilled or roasted meats or fish, or it can be served as a vegetarian main dish if you swap out the pancetta for poached eggs.

To roast the cauliflower, preheat the oven to 375°F. In a large bowl, toss the cauliflower with the oil. Spread the cauliflower in a single layer on a large sheet pan and season evenly with salt and pepper. Roast until the cauliflower begins to brown on its edges and is crisp-tender, about 25 minutes.

To make the vinaigrette, in a small bowl, whisk together the shallot, mustard, and vinegar. Slowly add the oil in a thin stream while whisking vigorously until emulsified. (The vinaigrette will keep in an airtight container in the refrigerator for up to 1 week.)

In a large skillet, warm the oil over medium heat. Add the pancetta and cook, stirring occasionally, until crunchy and browned, about 15 minutes. Add the cauliflower, tossing it with the pancetta, and heat, tossing and stirring, until warmed through, about 4 minutes. Add the vinaigrette and cook, stirring, until well combined, about 2 minutes. Set aside to cool slightly, about 10 minutes.

To assemble the salad, put the arugula into a large bowl. Add the cauliflower mixture to the arugula and toss to mix well. Divide the salad evenly among individual plates and serve at once.

WARM WILD MUSHROOM AND ARUGULA SALAD

WITH POACHED EGG AND TRUFFLE VINAIGRETTE

For the truffle vinaigrette:
3 tablespoons sherry vinegar
1 tablespoon Dijon mustard
1 shallot, minced (about 2 teaspoons)
Kosher salt and freshly ground
  black pepper
½ cup white truffle oil, or ¼ cup each
  white truffle oil and grapeseed oil

For the poached eggs:
1 tablespoon distilled white vinegar
4 to 6 large eggs

1 lb arugula
5 tablespoons unsalted butter
1 lb mixed wild mushrooms (such
  as chanterelle, king trumpet, black
  trumpet, and/or oyster), cleaned,
  stems ends trimmed, and torn
  into bite-size pieces
8 oz ham, rind removed and cut
  into ½-inch cubes
8 oz celery root, peeled and cut
  into matchsticks
¼ cup hazelnuts, toasted, skinned,
  and chopped
Kosher salt and freshly ground
  black pepper

Makes 4 to 6 servings

Our spin on the classic French *salade lyonnaise* replaces the lardons with smoky ham and the frisée with spicy arugula. A generous measure of wild mushrooms and an earthy truffle vinaigrette take this salad into another realm. Of course, the crowning jewel is the runny poached egg perched on top. The mix of mushroom varieties adds complex yet nuanced flavor. Be sure to use a large skillet so the mushrooms sear rather than steam. If you can't find hazelnuts, you can substitute chopped toasted walnuts or pecans.

To make the vinaigrette, in a small bowl, whisk together the sherry vinegar, mustard, shallot, and a pinch each of salt and pepper. Slowly add the oil in a thin stream while whisking vigorously until emulsified. Set aside.

To poach the eggs, line a medium, flat plate with a few paper towels and place the plate near the stove top. Pour water to a depth of about 2 inches into a large, wide pot or a large, deep sauté pan and bring to a boil over high heat. Reduce the heat to a simmer and add the vinegar. Crack each egg into a small bowl or ramekin. Holding a bowl so the lip just touches the water, gently tip the bowl to slide the egg into the water. Quickly repeat with the remaining eggs. Cook, using a slotted spoon to keep the eggs separated if necessary, until the whites are set and the yolks are still runny (medium), about 3½ minutes. Using the slotted spoon, transfer the eggs to the paper towels to drain.

Put the arugula into a large bowl. In a large sauté pan, melt the butter over medium-high heat. Add the mushrooms and cook, stirring, until soft, 4 to 5 minutes. Add the ham, celery root, and hazelnuts and sauté, tossing continuously, until heated through, about 1 minute longer. Add ½ cup of the vinaigrette and deglaze the pan, stirring to dislodge any browned bits from the pan bottom.

Quickly add the contents of the pan to the arugula and toss to combine. Season to taste with salt and pepper. Divide the salad evenly among four individual plates or bowls. Top each salad with a poached egg, sprinkle with salt and pepper, and serve at once. Pass the remaining vinaigrette at the table.

GRILLED ROMAINE SALAD

WITH LEMON-ANCHOVY VINAIGRETTE

For the lemon-anchovy vinaigrette:

⅓ cup fresh lemon juice (from about 3 lemons)

4 olive oil–packed anchovy fillets

2 cloves garlic, minced

1 tablespoon Dijon mustard

1 tablespoon grated Parmesan cheese

¼ teaspoon kosher salt

½ teaspoon freshly ground black pepper

¾ cup extra-virgin olive oil

1 tablespoon extra-virgin olive oil, plus more for brushing

½ cup fresh bread crumbs

4 small romaine hearts

Kosher salt

½ cup freshly grated Parmesan cheese

Makes 4 servings

Chef Mark Franz created this delicious salad for the opening menu of Nick's Cove in 2007. For years it was a guest favorite, and it still makes appearances on the menu from time to time. If you have never tried grilling romaine, get ready for a delightful surprise. The smoky depth of flavor, the slight wilt of the leaves, and the tangy, salty dressing are guaranteed to win over your dinner guests.

To make the vinaigrette, in a blender, combine the lemon juice, anchovies, garlic, mustard, Parmesan, salt, and pepper, and blend on medium-high speed until smooth. With the blender running, slowly drizzle in the oil, blending until the vinaigrette is emulsified. Set aside. (The vinaigrette will keep in an airtight container in the refrigerator for up to 4 days.)

In a dry small skillet, warm 1 tablespoon oil over medium heat. Add the bread crumbs and cook, stirring, until golden brown, about 4 minutes. Remove from the heat.

Prepare a charcoal or gas grill for direct cooking over medium-high heat. Brush the grill grate clean.

While the grill heats, halve each romaine heart lengthwise, then carefully cut away most of the core, leaving enough stem intact to keep the leaves attached. Brush the cut sides of the romaine lightly with the oil, then season with salt.

Arrange the romaine halves, cut side down, on the grate and grill just until the leaves are nicely charred, about 1½ minutes. You don't want to cook the romaine. You just want to create nice char marks.

Transfer two romaine halves, grilled side up, to each individual plate, arranging them in an X. Drizzle each serving with about ¼ cup of the vinaigrette, then sprinkle with 2 tablespoons bread crumbs and 2 tablespoons Parmesan. Serve at once.

WARM CHARD, CRANBERRY, AND ALMOND SALAD
WITH POACHED EGG AND BLUE CHEESE VINAIGRETTE

For the blue cheese vinaigrette:
4 oz mild blue cheese (such as Point Reyes Original Blue)
3 tablespoons cider vinegar
½ cup extra-virgin olive oil

For the poached eggs:
1 tablespoon distilled white vinegar
6 large eggs

2 bunches rainbow Swiss chard, stems and ribs removed and leaves cut into ½-inch-wide strips
1 cup salted roasted Marcona almonds
1 cup dried cranberries
6 oz mild blue cheese (such as Point Reyes Original Blue), crumbled

Makes 6 servings

Because of our coastal climate, our Croft produces an abundance of chard almost year-round. This recipe honors the hard work of our farmers in the very best way. Perfect for chilly autumn days, the warm salad makes a great lunch or a light dinner. Creamy pungent cheese, salty Marcona almonds, and tart cranberries add layers of texture and flavor. And who can resist a salad topped with a warm poached egg?

To make the vinaigrette, in a blender, combine the cheese, vinegar, and ⅓ cup water and blend on medium speed until smooth. With the blender running, slowly drizzle in the oil, blending until the vinaigrette is emulsified. Pour the vinaigrette into a small saucepan and set aside. (The vinaigrette will keep in an airtight container in the refrigerator for up to 3 days.)

To poach the eggs, line a large, flat plate with a few paper towels and place the plate near the stove top. Pour water to a depth of about 2 inches into a large, wide pot or a large, deep sauté pan and bring to a boil over high heat. Reduce the heat to a simmer and add the vinegar. Working in batches of three eggs, crack each egg into a small bowl or ramekin. Holding a bowl so the lip just touches the water, gently tip the bowl to slide the egg into the water. Quickly repeat with two more eggs. Cook, using a slotted spoon to keep them separated if necessary, until the whites are set and the yolks are still runny (medium), about 3½ minutes. Using the slotted spoon, transfer the eggs to the paper towels to drain. Repeat with the remaining eggs.

To assemble the salad, put the chard into a large bowl. Place the pan with the vinaigrette over medium heat and heat just until the dressing is warm, about 2 minutes. Pour the dressing over the chard and toss to coat evenly. Add the almonds and cranberries and toss to mix well. Divide the salad evenly among six individual bowls. Top each salad with 1 oz of blue cheese and a poached egg and serve at once.

FARRO AND HERBS
WITH GINGER-JALAPEÑO DRESSING

For the farro:
2½ cups pearled farro
¼ cup sliced green onions,
  green parts only
2 tablespoons minced shallot
2 tablespoons thinly sliced
  fresh mint leaves
2 tablespoons thinly sliced
  fresh basil leaves
2 tablespoons thinly sliced
  fresh cilantro leaves
¼ cup chopped roasted cashews
8 oz arugula

For the ginger-jalapeño dressing:
¼ cup low-sodium soy sauce
1 small jalapeño chile, seeded,
  deveined, and minced
2 tablespoons peeled and minced
  fresh ginger
2 teaspoons Asian fish sauce
2 teaspoons toasted sesame oil
Kosher salt

Makes 4 to 6 servings

Nutty *farro* and the bright, fresh flavors of mint, cilantro, and basil marry perfectly with the spicy kick of this flavorful dressing. Fresh ginger and fish sauce give the dressing a surprising Southeast Asian accent. At the restaurant, we serve this salad as an entrée in a big bowl, and guests may add fish, shrimp, or chicken to it.

Rinse the farro under cold running water and drain well. Bring a large pot filled with salted water to a boil, add the farro, reduce the heat to medium, and cook uncovered, skimming any foam that forms on the surface, until the farro is tender, about 20 minutes. Drain, rinse under cold running water to stop the cooking, and then drain well.

Transfer the farro to a medium bowl, cover, and refrigerate until chilled, about 1 hour. You should have about 5 cups cooked farro.

In a large bowl, combine the chilled farro, green onions, shallot, mint, basil, cilantro, cashews, and arugula and stir and toss to mix well.

To make the dressing, in a blender, combine ¼ cup water, the soy sauce, jalapeño, ginger, fish sauce, and sesame oil and blend on medium speed until well mixed. Season to taste with salt. (The vinaigrette will keep in an airtight container in the refrigerator for up to 3 days.)

Drizzle the dressing over the farro mixture and stir until evenly coated, then serve. The salad can also sit at room temperature for up to 1 hour or in the refrigerator for up to 1 day before serving.

SPICY SUGGESTION

The addition of a whole jalapeño in the dressing gives it a spicy kick. But if that's not your thing, feel free to only use half or a quarter of the chile depending on your spice tolerance.

SHRIMP LOUIE SALAD

For the Louie dressing:
½ cup mayonnaise
¼ cup ketchup
¼ cup sour cream
Juice of ½ lemon
Dash of vinegar-based hot sauce
  (such as Tabasco)

For the shrimp:
½ small white onion, roughly
  chopped
1 celery stalk, roughly chopped
1 clove garlic, roughly chopped
1 lemon, halved
2 bay leaves
¼ cup kosher salt
1 tablespoon black peppercorns
20 large shrimp in the shell, about
  1 lb, peeled and deveined

4 large eggs
2 small heads butter lettuce, leaves
  separated
2 Roma tomatoes, halved, seeded,
  and finely chopped
2 radishes, trimmed and thinly sliced
2 small avocados, halved, pitted,
  peeled, and thinly sliced

Makes 4 servings

A Nick's Cove classic, our shrimp Louie is all about the presentation: a "bowl" of butter lettuce leaves filled with diced tomato, sieved egg yolk and chopped egg white, perfectly ripe sliced avocado, and plenty of shrimp. If you have access to Dungeness crab, feel free to substitute 1 lb of fresh-cooked crabmeat in place of the shrimp. If you simply cannot choose between the two, a combo of shrimp and crab is a great option, too. When we aren't growing butter lettuce in the Croft, we purchase "living" hydroponic heads with the roots attached, as they are the freshest lettuce available in the off-season. Staff secret: The Louie dressing is the ideal dipping sauce for fries!

To make the dressing, in a small bowl, whisk together all of the ingredients until well mixed. Cover and refrigerate for at least 30 minutes before using. (The dressing will keep in an airtight container in the refrigerator for up to 3 days.)

To poach the shrimp, fill a large bowl half full with water and ice. In a large pot, combine the onion, celery, garlic, lemon, bay leaves, salt, peppercorns, and 3 qt water and bring to a boil over high heat, stirring to dissolve the salt. Add the shrimp, adjust the heat to maintain a gentle simmer, and cook the shrimp until they turn pink and are opaque and cooked through, about 6 minutes. Using a slotted spoon, transfer the shrimp to the ice bath.

To hard-boil the eggs, return the shrimp cooking water to a boil, carefully add the eggs, and cook at a slow boil for 13 minutes. Meanwhile, remove the shrimp from the ice bath and pat dry, then add a few more ice cubes to the bowl. When the eggs are ready, using the slotted spoon, transfer the eggs to the ice bath. When the eggs are cool, peel them, cut them in half, and separate the yolks from the whites. Finely chop the egg whites and set the yolks aside.

To assemble the salads, divide the lettuce leaves evenly among four individual plates, arranging them so they create a "bowl" on the plate. Place five poached shrimp in the center of each salad. Divide the egg whites, tomatoes, and radishes evenly among the salads, arranging them in separate piles. Using one egg yolk for each salad, press it through a fine-mesh sieve, distributing it evenly over the top. Drizzle about ¼ cup of the dressing over each salad. Place an avocado half on each salad, fanning the slices neatly. Serve the salads at once, passing any remaining dressing at the table.

Coast Miwok

The Coast Miwok, one of four linguistically linked Miwok bands indigenous to Northern California, were hunter-gatherers native to Marin and southern Sonoma County. From the land they gathered plants, berries, nuts, and seeds and hunted fowl, deer, elk, and rabbits. Each year, they would migrate west to take advantage of the pristine waters of Tomales Bay during peak fishing season, camping along the bay in the area now known as Nick's Cove. Whether it was from the animals they hunted or the sea life they caught, they wasted nothing: pelts for warmth, antlers for arrowheads, shells for ornaments and currency.

I see parallels in what we strive to do at Nick's Cove and the life of the original Coast Miwok. They lived farm-to-table in the most authentic sense of the term, and at Nick's Cove we endeavor to continue in that same tradition. Whenever possible, we choose sustainably raised and humanely harvested meats and sustainably raised and caught seafood, and we enjoy produce grown in the Croft, our on-site farm (see page 68). Today, descendants of the Coast Miwok live throughout the Bay Area, and their age-old traditions continue to inspire us.

A Coast Miwok roundhouse entrance at Miwok Indian Village.

PORCINI AND WHITE TRUFFLE CREAM SOUP

For the stock:
2 oz dried porcini mushrooms
2 oz dried shiitake mushrooms
½ large yellow onion, chopped
1 celery stalk, chopped
1 tablespoon chopped fresh thyme
5 black peppercorns
1 bay leaf

¼ cup extra-virgin olive oil
2 large leeks, white parts only,
  finely chopped
1 yellow onion, finely chopped
2 celery stalks, finely chopped
2 large cloves garlic, chopped
1 cup dry white wine
¾ cup jasmine rice
1 bay leaf
2 cups heavy cream
2 tablespoons minced fresh
  thyme leaves
1 tablespoon kosher salt
⅛ teaspoon freshly grated nutmeg
Freshly ground black pepper
1 oz Italian winter white truffles,
  or 2 tablespoons white truffle oil

Makes 6 servings

With their woodsy aroma, porcini mushrooms add deep flavor to this delicate cream-based soup. This soup makes an elegant first course for a dinner party, but it is equally at home at a casual Sunday meal with family and friends. I like to serve it with a freshly baked loaf of seeded wheat bread and herbed butter.

To make the stock, in a large pot, combine the dried mushrooms, onion, celery, thyme, peppercorns, bay leaf, and 3 qt water and bring to a simmer over medium-high heat. Reduce the heat to low and simmer for 1 hour. Turn off the heat and let the stock cool to room temperature. Strain through a fine-mesh sieve into a clean container and discard the solids. You should have about 8 cups stock. (The stock can be stored in an airtight container in the refrigerator for up to 1 week.)

To make the soup, in a large saucepan, warm the oil over low heat. Add the leeks, onion, and celery and cook, stirring, until the vegetables soften, about 5 minutes. Add the garlic and cook, stirring, until it begins to soften, 2 to 3 minutes. Pour in the wine, stir well, and cook until reduced by half, 5 to 7 minutes. Increase the heat to medium, add the reserved mushroom stock, rice, and bay leaf, and bring to a simmer. Cover and simmer, stirring occasionally and adjusting the heat as needed to maintain a simmer, until the rice is tender, 30 to 35 minutes.

Discard the bay leaf, then stir in the cream, thyme, salt, and nutmeg and season to taste with pepper. Remove from the heat. In batches, puree the soup in a blender, then return to the pot. Return the pot to medium-low heat and warm just until piping hot.

To serve, divide the soup evenly among six individual bowls. If you have fresh truffles, using a truffle peeler or a sharp vegetable peeler, shave an equal amount over each bowl. If using truffle oil, drizzle about 1 teaspoon over each bowl. Serve at once.

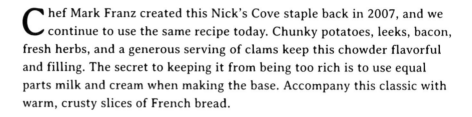

TOMALES BAY CLAM CHOWDER

6 thick-cut slices applewood-smoked
   bacon (about 10 oz), cut into
   1-inch pieces
1 large yellow onion, finely chopped
1 large leek, white and pale green
   parts, finely chopped
2 celery stalks, finely chopped
3 large russet potatoes, peeled and
   cut into ¾-inch cubes
4 cans (6 oz each) chopped clams
   with juice
2 cups bottled clam juice
2 teaspoons fresh thyme leaves,
   minced
1 bay leaf
½ teaspoon freshly ground black
   pepper

For the béchamel:
4 tablespoons unsalted butter
⅓ cup all-purpose flour
1 cup whole milk
1 cup heavy cream
½ teaspoon kosher salt
⅛ teaspoon freshly grated nutmeg

¼ cup chopped fresh flat-leaf parsley
   leaves, for garnish

Makes 6 servings

Chef Mark Franz created this Nick's Cove staple back in 2007, and we continue to use the same recipe today. Chunky potatoes, leeks, bacon, fresh herbs, and a generous serving of clams keep this chowder flavorful and filling. The secret to keeping it from being too rich is to use equal parts milk and cream when making the base. Accompany this classic with warm, crusty slices of French bread.

In a large pot, cook half of the bacon over medium heat, stirring occasionally, until beginning to brown, about 7 minutes. Add the onion, leek, and celery and cook, stirring occasionally, until the vegetables start to soften, about 7 minutes. Add the potatoes and stir to combine. Add the clams with their juice, the clam juice, thyme, bay leaf, and pepper. Bring to a simmer and cook, stirring occasionally, until the potatoes are tender, 25 to 30 minutes. Remove from the heat and cover to keep warm.

While the potatoes cook, make the béchamel. In a heavy medium saucepan, melt the butter over medium heat. Add the flour and whisk until smooth, then cook, stirring constantly, until the mixture bubbles and smells of shortbread, about 1 minute. While whisking constantly, slowly add the milk, continuing to whisk until the mixture is smooth. Bring to a boil, whisking occasionally, then reduce the heat to low and cook, stirring, until thickened, 3 to 5 minutes.

Stir in the cream, increase the heat to medium, and bring to a gentle simmer. Add the salt and nutmeg and cook, stirring until slightly thickened, about 10 minutes.

Meanwhile, line a large plate with paper towels. In a medium skillet, cook the remaining bacon over medium-high heat, stirring occasionally, until browned and crisp, about 10 minutes. Using a slotted spoon, transfer to the towel-lined plate to drain. Reserve for garnish.

When the béchamel is ready, add it to the clam-potato mixture and stir to combine. If the chowder has cooled, reheat gently over medium-low heat, stirring often to prevent scorching, until piping hot. Remove the bay leaf. Divide the chowder evenly among six individual bowls. Garnish each serving with the parsley and bacon, dividing them evenly, and serve at once.

NICK'S COVE CIOPPINO

For the broth:
¼ cup extra-virgin olive oil
1 large red onion, finely chopped
1 small fennel bulb, trimmed, cored, and finely chopped
2 celery stalks, finely chopped
3 cloves garlic, minced
2 cups dry white wine
2 teaspoons smoked paprika
1 teaspoon red pepper flakes
1 teaspoon dried thyme
1 bay leaf
3 cups bottled clam juice or fish stock
1 (28-oz) can diced tomatoes, with juices
Kosher salt and freshly ground black pepper

For the crostini:
1 loaf French baguette
3 tablespoons extra-virgin olive oil
Kosher salt

For the seafood:
2 tablespoons unsalted butter
1 lb medium shrimp in the shell, peeled and deveined
1 Dungeness crab, freshly cooked and cracked (optional; page 92)
18 to 20 medium mussels, scrubbed clean and beards removed
18 to 20 small Manila clams
3 rock cod fillets, 8 oz each, halved crosswise

2 lemons, quartered
Leaves from 1 bunch flat-leaf parsley, chopped

Makes 6 to 8 servings

Cioppino is one of those San Francisco staples that relies heavily on great seafood, and our version does not disappoint. The richly flavored broth provides a silky base for a profusion of shrimp, crab, mussels, clams, and fish. It takes a bit of patience and one eye on the clock to make a great cioppino, but the result is well worth the effort. Be sure to serve it with the crunchy crostini prepared here or with crusty slices of sourdough bread.

To make the broth, in a large pot, warm the oil over medium heat. Add the onion, fennel, celery, and garlic and cook, stirring, until the vegetables are slightly softened, about 5 minutes. Add the wine, paprika, pepper flakes, thyme, and bay leaf and cook, stirring occasionally, until the wine is reduced by about half, about 10 minutes. Pour in the clam juice and tomatoes with their juices and simmer, stirring occasionally, until fragrant, about 15 minutes.

Remove from the heat and discard the bay leaf. Using an immersion blender, lightly puree the mixture, so it is still slightly chunky. (Alternatively, in batches, puree the mixture in a blender, then return to the pot.) Season to taste with salt, black pepper, and more pepper flakes if needed. Return the pot to the stove top, cover, and keep warm on the lowest heat setting.

To make the crostini, preheat the oven to 350°F. Cut the bread on a sharp diagonal into long slices each about ½ inch thick. Arrange the slices in a single layer on a sheet pan, brush both sides with the oil, and sprinkle with salt. Toast, turning once halfway through and checking to make sure the slices are not getting too dark, until crisp and golden brown, 8 to 10 minutes. Set aside.

If necessary, reheat the broth over low heat until piping hot. To cook the seafood, in a large skillet, melt the butter over medium heat. Add the shrimp, crab (if using), mussels and clams (discarding any that fail to close to the touch), and fish and cook, stirring gently, for 2 to 3 minutes. Add the seafood to the hot broth, then cover the pot and steam, stirring gently every so often, until the mussels and clams have opened, the shrimp have turned pink and are opaque and cooked through, and the crab is heated through, about 5 minutes. Discard any clams or mussels that failed to open.

Divide the seafood evenly among shallow bowls, then add about 2 ladlefuls of the hot broth to each bowl. Garnish each serving with crostini, a lemon wedge, and generous sprinkling of parsley. Serve at once.

DUNGENESS CRAB MAC AND CHEESE

1 cup unsalted butter

2 leeks, white parts only, sliced

¾ cup all-purpose flour

3 cups whole milk

3 cups heavy cream

2 cups shredded aged Gruyère cheese, such as Gran Cru

2 cups shredded Point Reyes Toma or medium white Cheddar

½ cup grated Parmesan cheese

Kosher salt

Vinegar-based hot sauce (such as Tabasco), for seasoning

Juice of ¼ lemon

1 lb dried fusilli pasta

1 tablespoon extra-virgin olive oil

½ cup fresh bread crumbs

1 lb fresh-cooked Dungeness crabmeat, picked over for shell fragments (page 92)

2 tablespoons chopped fresh flat-leaf parsley leaves

Makes 6 to 8 servings

While our crab mac and cheese is the ultimate in decadence, it also speaks to the kid in all of us. It's creamy and rich with three kinds of cheese, plus we make sure every bite includes plenty of Dungeness crab. The toasted bread crumbs on top add amazing texture and crunch to the finished dish. This recipe is so good it goes fast once it's on the table, so you should consider making a double batch. When crab is out of season, you can serve the mac and cheese plain or you can mix in a drizzle of truffle oil or some crumbled cooked bacon.

In a large, heavy saucepan, melt the butter over medium heat. Add the leeks and cook, stirring occasionally, until softened, 5 to 7 minutes. Add the flour, whisk until smooth, then cook, stirring constantly, until the mixture bubbles and starts to smell of shortbread, 2 to 3 minutes. Slowly add the milk, continuing to stir until the mixture is smooth and comes to a boil. Reduce the heat to low and simmer, stirring, until slightly thickened, about 5 minutes. Stir in the cream. Continue to simmer, stirring, until the mixture begins to thicken, about 5 minutes. Add the Gruyère, Toma, and Parmesan, a handful at a time, stirring after each addition until melted before adding more. Season to taste with salt, hot sauce, and lemon juice.

About 15 minutes before the cheese sauce is ready, begin cooking the pasta and toast the bread crumbs. Fill a large pot two-thirds full with salted water and bring to a boil over high heat. Add the pasta and cook, stirring occasionally, until al dente, 6 to 8 minutes or according to package directions. Drain into a colander, shake the colander to force out any excess moisture, and transfer to a large bowl. Keep warm.

In a dry small skillet, warm the oil over medium heat. Add the bread crumbs and cook, stirring, until golden brown, about 4 minutes. Remove from the heat.

Pour the cheese sauce over the pasta and stir to mix. Add the crabmeat and stir gently to distribute evenly. Divide the pasta among individual bowls or plates. Top each serving with the toasted bread crumbs and parsley, dividing evenly. Serve at once.

CLEANING & COOKING CRAB

You can buy a live crab and cook it yourself by immersing it in boiling water for 10 to 15 minutes, depending on its size, or you can buy a freshly cooked crab. To crack the crab, place it, shell side down, on a work surface and lift off and discard the apron (triangular tail flap). Flip the crab over and lift off and discard the large top shell. The pale yellow crab fat in the shell can be scooped and reserved for enriching sauces or discarded. Remove the gray, feathery gills on both sides of the body, the brownish organs in the center, and the jaw section at the front and discard them all. Twist off the claws and legs and cut or break the body into quarters. Rinse all the pieces under cold water.

Serve as cracked crab with plenty of melted butter and lemon, or use in a recipe such as Nick's Cove Cioppino (page 88). At the table, provide crab or lobster crackers or nutcrackers for cracking the claws and legs so guests can extract the meat. Or, crack each piece and extract the meat to use in recipes like Dungeness Crab Mac and Cheese (page 90) or Dungeness Crab Benedict (page 95).

DUNGENESS CRAB BENEDICT

For the hollandaise:
⅔ cup dry white wine
1 bay leaf
5 black peppercorns
1 tablespoon Champagne vinegar
1 cup unsalted butter
3 large egg yolks
1 teaspoon kosher salt
Dash of hot sauce

For the poached eggs:
1 tablespoon distilled white vinegar
8 large eggs

For the Benedicts:
2 avocados
4 English muffins, split
2 tablespoons unsalted butter
1 lb fresh-cooked Dungeness
  crabmeat, picked over for shell
  fragments (page 92)
2 teaspoons smoked paprika

Makes 4 servings

Dungeness crab is plentiful in Tomales Bay and nearby Bodega Bay, so it makes perfect sense to add fresh crabmeat to a decadent Benedict. As a result, it is one of the most ordered dishes on our menu. If you decide to crack the crab and pick the crabmeat on your own for this recipe, be sure to choose a crab with a deep-colored shell, and give one of the legs a quick squeeze to make sure it's hardy rather than flimsy. Limp legs and thin shells are a sign of recent molting, which means the crab won't contain as much meat.

To make the hollandaise, in a small saucepan, combine the wine, bay leaf, peppercorns, and vinegar and bring to a boil over medium-high heat. Reduce the heat to medium-low and simmer gently until the liquid is reduced to about 2 tablespoons, about 8 minutes. Remove from the heat and let steep for 10 minutes. Strain through a fine-mesh sieve into a small bowl and set aside.

Return the saucepan to the stove top, add the butter, and melt over medium heat. Remove from the heat and let sit for 5 minutes to allow the milk solids to settle to the bottom of the pan. Carefully pour the clear yellow liquid—this is the clarified butter—into a measuring cup, leaving behind only the milk solids in the pan; discard the milk solids.

Pour water to a depth of about 2 inches into a medium saucepan and bring to a gentle simmer over medium heat. Rest a heatproof medium bowl on top of the saucepan over (not touching) the water. Add the egg yolks, wine reduction, and salt to the bowl and whisk until blended, then continue to whisk constantly until the mixture begins to thicken, 3 to 4 minutes. Remove from the heat and gradually add the clarified butter, about 2 tablespoons at a time, while whisking constantly. The sauce should be smooth and thick; if it is too thick, whisk in 1 tablespoon warm water. Whisk in the hot sauce. Return the bowl to over the saucepan off the heat, cover to keep warm, and set aside.

To poach the eggs, line a large, flat plate with a few paper towels and place the plate near the stove top. Pour water to a depth of about 2 inches into a large, wide pot or a large, deep sauté pan and bring to a boil over high heat. Reduce the heat to a simmer and add the vinegar. Working in batches of four eggs, crack each egg into a small bowl or ramekin. Holding a bowl so the lip just touches the water, gently tip the bowl to slide the egg into the water. Quickly repeat with three more eggs. Cook, using a slotted spoon to keep them separated if necessary, until the whites are set and the yolks are still runny (medium), about 3½ minutes. Using

continued . . .

the slotted spoon, transfer the eggs to the paper towels to drain. Repeat with the remaining eggs.

While the eggs are cooking, preheat the broiler. Cut each avocado in half lengthwise, discard the pit, and then, using a metal spoon, carefully scoop out each half from the skin. Place the avocado halves, cut side down, on a cutting board and thinly slice lengthwise, keeping the shape of each half intact.

When the broiler is ready, arrange the English muffins, cut side up, on a sheet pan, slide under the broiler, and toast until light brown, about 3 minutes.

To assemble the eggs Benedict, place two toasted muffin halves, cut side up, on each of four individual plates. Top each muffin half with one-fourth of an avocado, fanning the slices neatly.

In a medium saucepan, melt the butter over medium-high heat. Add the crab and heat, stirring occasionally, just until warmed through, 2 to 3 minutes. Top each muffin half with about 3 tablespoons of the warm crab, spooning the crab on top of the avocado. Next, place a poached egg on top of each mound of crab and spoon about 2 tablespoons of the warm hollandaise over each egg. Dust each serving with about ½ teaspoon of the paprika. Serve at once.

LOBSTER POUTINE

2 uncooked lobster tails, about
  8 oz each
1 celery stalk, chopped
½ small yellow onion, chopped
1 small carrot, chopped
1 bay leaf

For the béchamel:
4 tablespoons unsalted butter
¼ cup all-purpose flour
2 cups whole milk
½ teaspoon Old Bay or similar
  seafood seasoning
Kosher salt

4 tablespoons unsalted butter
Cooked hand-cut fries, homemade
  (page 59) or store-bought
  (2-lb package)
8 oz creamy pungent cheese (such
  as Nicasio Square or Taleggio)

Makes 4 to 6 servings

Here is our take on poutine, a hearty, wildly popular Canadian dish that originated in Quebec Province and soon spread across the Great White North. Our version calls for sweet lobster, rich gravy, and crispy fries. Putting it together takes a bit of work, but the indulgent result makes it all worthwhile. If you can't find lobster, a pound of fresh-cooked Dungeness crabmeat transforms it into a wonderful California-inspired variation.

To prepare the lobster, using kitchen shears, cut lengthwise along the middle of the back of each lobster tail, and then cut lengthwise along the middle of the underside of the tail. Pull the shell halves apart, exposing the meat and setting the shells aside. Remove the meat and cut into ½-inch cubes. Put the meat into an airtight container and refrigerate until ready to use.

To make the stock, in a medium pot, combine the lobster shells, celery, onion, carrot, bay leaf, and 8 cups water and bring to a simmer over medium-high heat. Simmer rapidly for 30 minutes, then reduce the heat to low, cover partially, and gently simmer for 1 hour.

Remove from the heat and strain through a fine-mesh sieve into a saucepan. Place the saucepan over medium-high heat, bring to a boil, and cook until reduced to about 1 cup. Remove from the heat and pour into a heatproof measuring cup. Set aside.

To make the béchamel, rinse out the saucepan used for the stock, place over medium-high heat, and add the 4 tablespoons butter. When the butter melts, slowly whisk in the flour until the mixture is smooth, then continue to whisk until a thick roux forms, about 2 minutes. The roux should be light brown. While whisking constantly, slowly add ⅔ cup of the lobster stock, continuing to whisk until the mixture is smooth and has thickened. Pour in the milk while whisking constantly, then reduce the heat to medium-low and continue to cook, stirring, until a thick béchamel forms, about 4 minutes. Add the seafood seasoning and then season with salt to taste. Remove from the heat. Any leftover lobster stock can be frozen for future use.

In a skillet, melt the 4 tablespoons butter. Add the lobster pieces and cook, stirring occasionally, until they turn opaque but are tender, 3 to 4 minutes. Set aside.

If making the hand-cut fries, immerse the cooked fries in oil heated to 350°F to re-crisp the fries. If using store-bought fries, cook them according to the package directions.

Mound the hot fries on a large serving platter. Break up the cheese, crumbling it over the top. Pour all of the béchamel over the cheese, then top with the buttery lobster pieces. Serve right away.

SHRIMP ENCHILADAS

WITH SALSA VERDE AND SALSA ROJA

For the cilantro crema:
½ cup sour cream
2 tablespoons finely chopped
  fresh cilantro
1½ tablespoons fresh lemon juice
1 teaspoon kosher salt

For the salsa roja:
2 tablespoons extra-virgin olive oil
1 large yellow onion, finely chopped
2 large cloves garlic, minced
1 small jalapeño chile, seeded
  and minced
2 teaspoons ground cumin
1 bay leaf
1 (14½-oz) can diced tomatoes
  with juice
Kosher salt

For the salsa verde:
2 tablespoons extra-virgin olive oil
1 large yellow onion, finely chopped
2 large cloves garlic, minced
1 small jalapeño chile, seeded
  and minced
1 teaspoon ground cumin
¼ cup chopped fresh cilantro
1 (16-oz) can whole tomatillos,
  drained and chopped
Kosher salt

ingredients continued . . .

Our cooks are often in charge of our family-style staff meals, and when shrimp enchiladas ended up as a meal one day, we knew they were just too good not to share with our guests, so we put them on the menu. Now they are so popular that they can never come off. We serve the enchiladas with two sauces, red and green, but you can choose to serve it with just one, if you like. If you make the *crema* and sauces a day in advance, they will taste even better, as their flavors will have had time to develop. Plus, it will save you time when you are ready to assemble the dish.

To make the crema, in a small bowl, whisk together the sour cream, cilantro, lemon juice, and salt until well mixed. Cover and refrigerate for at least 1 hour. The crema will keep for up to 5 days, but it tastes best made a day in advance of using.

To make the salsa roja, in a medium saucepan, warm the olive oil over medium heat. Add the onion and cook, stirring, until it begins to soften, about 4 minutes. Add the garlic and chile and cook, stirring, until beginning to soften, about 1 minute. Add the cumin and bay leaf and stir to mix, then add the tomatoes and their juice, ½ cup water, and a large pinch of salt. Bring the mixture to a boil, then reduce the heat to low and simmer, uncovered, until all of the vegetables are soft and the flavors are blended, about 15 minutes. Remove from the heat, discard the bay leaf, and let cool for a few minutes.

Transfer the contents of the pan to a blender or food processor and process until smooth. Let cool completely. You should have about 2 cups. The salsa will keep in an airtight container in the refrigerator for up to 5 days, but it tastes best made a day in advance of using.

To make the salsa verde, in a medium saucepan, warm the olive oil over medium heat. Add the onion and cook, stirring, until it begins to soften, about 4 minutes. Add the garlic and chile and cook, stirring, until beginning to soften, about 1 minute. Add the cumin and cilantro and stir to mix, then add the tomatillos, ¾ cup water, and a large pinch of salt. Bring the mixture to a boil, then reduce the heat to low and simmer, uncovered, until all the vegetables are soft and the flavors are blended, about 15 minutes. Remove from the heat and let cool for a few minutes.

Transfer the contents of the pan to the blender or food processor and process until smooth. Let cool completely. You should have about 2 cups. The salsa will keep in an airtight container in the refrigerator for up to 5 days, but it tastes best made a day in advance of using.

continued . . .

½ cup canola oil

½ small yellow onion, finely chopped

1½ lb medium shrimp in the shell,
   peeled and deveined

1 clove garlic, minced

1 tablespoon smoked paprika

1 teaspoon ground cumin

½ teaspoon red pepper flakes

¼ cup dry white wine

½ cup mascarpone cheese

⅓ cup crumbled cotija cheese,
   plus more for garnish

2 tablespoons finely chopped
   fresh cilantro

Kosher salt

8 flour tortillas, each about
   8 inches in diameter

Finely chopped fresh chives or
   cilantro, for garnish

Makes 4 servings

In a large skillet, warm ¼ cup of the canola oil over medium heat. Add the onion and cook, stirring, for 2 minutes. Then add the shrimp, garlic, paprika, cumin, and pepper flakes and cook, stirring occasionally, until the shrimp turn pink and are opaque and cooked through, about 3 minutes. Pour in the wine and simmer until some of the liquid cooks off, 2 to 3 minutes. Transfer the mixture to a heatproof medium bowl and let cool to room temperature.

Add the mascarpone, cotija, and 2 tablespoons cilantro to the cooled shrimp mixture and stir to mix well. Season to taste with salt.

Preheat the oven to 350°F. Spray an 8-inch square baking dish with nonstick cooking spray.

Lay a kitchen towel on a work surface. Warm a medium skillet over medium heat. When the pan is hot, add the tortillas, one at a time, and heat, flipping once, until warmed through, 20 to 30 seconds on each side. Do not allow them to brown and crisp. As the tortillas are ready, transfer them to one end of the towel and cover with the other end to keep warm.

While the tortillas are still warm, lay them out in a single layer on a work surface. Divide the filling evenly among the tortillas, spooning it in a slightly off-center line from one end of the tortilla to the other. Roll up each tortilla into a cylinder, enclosing the filling. Transfer the filled tortillas, seam side down, to the prepared baking dish.

Spoon 1 cup of the salsa verde evenly over four enchiladas. Spoon 1 cup of the salsa roja evenly over the remaining four enchiladas. Bake until the sauce browns and the enchiladas are warmed through, 15 to 20 minutes.

To serve, place one enchilada with salsa roja and one enchilada with salsa verde on each individual plate. Top the enchiladas with the cilantro crema, chives or cilantro, and a sprinkle of cotija cheese. Place any remaining salsa roja and salsa verde on the table for diners to add to their enchiladas as they like.

TUNA MELTS

WITH ROASTED TOMATOES AND THYME

For the tuna salad:
4 (5-oz) cans albacore tuna
  in water, drained
⅔ cup mayonnaise
1 large celery stalk, finely chopped
½ cup golden raisins
1 tablespoon Dijon mustard

For the roasted tomato puree:
4 large Roma tomatoes,
  quartered lengthwise
1 tablespoon minced fresh
  thyme leaves
1 teaspoon kosher salt
2 tablespoons extra-virgin olive oil
2 cloves garlic, minced

4 large slices brioche bread, each
  about 1 inch thick
4 large slices medium-sharp white
  Cheddar cheese (about 1 oz each
  and large enough to cover the
  bread slice)

Makes 4 servings

Tuna melts are one of my all-time-favorite comfort foods, and our version has all the requirements: creamy tuna salad, toasted bread, and melted Cheddar. But, like with many dishes at Nick's Cove, we like to take it one step further. Our tuna melts are served open-faced on buttery brioche with roasted tomato puree. Serve these luscious hot sandwiches with a simple green salad for a memorable lunch.

To make the tuna salad, in a medium bowl, combine the tuna, mayonnaise, celery, raisins, and mustard and stir gently, breaking up any large chunks of tuna, until well mixed. Cover and refrigerate until ready to use. (The tuna salad will keep in an airtight container in the refrigerator for up to 3 days.)

To make the tomato puree, preheat the oven to 350°F. Line a sheet pan with parchment paper. Place the tomatoes, cut side up, on the prepared pan. Sprinkle evenly with the thyme and salt and drizzle with the oil.

Roast the tomatoes until they start to soften, about 15 minutes. Remove from the oven, sprinkle evenly with the garlic, and then return to the oven and continue to roast until the tomatoes start to caramelize and the edges begin to char, about 20 minutes longer. Remove from oven and let cool on the pan on a wire rack for about 10 minutes. Increase the oven temperature to 375°F.

Transfer the tomatoes to a food processor, add ¼ cup water, and process to a smooth puree. Taste and adjust the seasoning with salt if needed.

To assemble the sandwiches, arrange the bread slices in a single layer on a sheet pan. Spread each bread slice evenly with 2 tablespoons of the tomato puree. Spoon one-fourth of the tuna salad (about 1 cup) onto each slice and then top with a slice of cheese (it should cover the top completely).

Bake the sandwiches until the cheese melts and the tuna is warmed through, about 10 minutes. Serve at once.

LOCAL SEAFOOD & FISHERMEN

Fishing in Tomales Bay has been a way of life since the area was first inhabited by the Coast Miwok Indians. Despite being hard, labor-intensive work, fishing for a living has provided livelihoods for many locals since that time.

Thanks to families like Andy and Mike Matkovich (the Matkovich brothers), Nick and Frances Kojich, and other Eastern European immigrants (see page 18), who found comfort in the familiarity of the land that resembled their homes along the Adriatic, fishing grew into a well-established industry in the early twentieth century and remained healthy until its decline in the 1970s.

Today, due to the efforts of environmentalists and conservation groups, the waters in Tomales Bay remain some of the most pristine in California. They are perfect not only for commercial fishermen but also for anyone who—like my husband—likes to spend a day on the bay setting out crab pots while enjoying a picnic on the western shore. The bay also offers the ideal temperature and level of salinity for growing oysters, a local favorite.

Oyster production in the area began in the early 1900s, when Tomales Bay Oyster Company (see page 36) began operations in 1909. Nowadays, oyster farming is thriving,

with Hog Island Oyster Company, Bodega Bay Oysters, Tomales Bay Oyster Company, and other smaller operations all turning out the prized shellfish.

While Nick's Cove makes good use of the oysters grown locally, we also bring in the bivalves from Drakes Bay Oyster Company in Baja California (formerly located in Drakes Bay), and from the Oregon coast. We want the experience of enjoying oysters to be as many different varieties as we can offer, both locally and from afar.

View of the oyster beds in southern Tomales Bay.

CHIPOTLE FISH TACOS

WITH PICO DE GALLO AND CILANTRO-LIME AIOLI

For the marinated fish:
½ cup fresh orange juice
½ bunch fresh cilantro
1 tablespoon chopped chipotle
  chile in adobo
1 small shallot, minced
1 clove garlic, minced
1½ teaspoons kosher salt
1 teaspoon ground cumin
1 teaspoon smoked paprika
2 lb rock cod fillets

For the cilantro-lime aioli:
3 large egg yolks
½ bunch cilantro, roughly chopped
1 celery stalk, roughly chopped
1 green onion, white and green
  parts, roughly chopped
1 clove garlic, roughly chopped
Juice of 2 limes
1 teaspoon kosher salt
¼ cup extra-virgin olive oil

For the pico de gallo:
8 large Roma tomatoes
¼ red onion, minced
Leaves from ½ bunch cilantro,
  minced
Juice of 2 limes
1 clove garlic, minced
½ teaspoon kosher salt

8 small white corn tortillas, each
  about 3 inches in diameter
1 tablespoon canola oil
½ small head green cabbage, cored
  and finely shredded
2 limes, quartered

Makes 4 servings

We marinate delicate, fresh rock cod in sweet orange juice and smoky chipotle chiles in adobo before searing it and finishing it in the oven. Layered on top of a warm corn tortilla and topped with our creamy cilantro-lime aioli, these fish tacos are simple to make, layered with flavor, and a definite crowd-pleaser. Don't forgo the sauce: anyone who knows fish tacos knows that it's all about the sauce!

To marinate the fish, in a blender, combine ½ cup water, the orange juice, cilantro, chile, shallot, garlic, salt, cumin, and paprika and blend on high speed to a smooth puree. Cut the fish into 1-inch-wide strips and transfer to a large bowl. Pour the marinade over the top and stir gently to coat the fish completely. Cover and refrigerate for at least 1 hour or up to 4 hours.

To make the aioli, rinse out the blender canister and return it to its base. Add ¼ cup water, the egg yolks, cilantro, celery, green onion, garlic, lime juice, and salt to the blender and blend on medium speed until smooth. With the blender running, slowly drizzle in the oil, blending until the mixture is emulsified. Transfer to an airtight container and refrigerate until ready to use or up to 5 days.

To make the pico de gallo, halve the tomatoes lengthwise and, holding the halves over the sink, squeeze out the seeds. Finely chop the tomatoes and transfer to a medium bowl. Add the onion, cilantro, lime juice, garlic, and salt and stir to mix. Cover and refrigerate until ready to use. (The pico de gallo can be made up to 1 day in advance.)

Preheat the oven to 350°F. Arrange the tortillas on a sheet pan in four stacks of two tortillas each.

In a large ovenproof skillet, warm the canola oil over medium-high heat. Remove the fish from the marinade, allowing any excess marinade to drip back into the bowl. Add the fish to the skillet and sear on the first side until golden, about 2 minutes. Turn and cook on the second side until golden, about 2 minutes.

Add ¼ cup water to the pan, then transfer the pan to the oven and cook until the fish is opaque and cooked through, 3 to 4 minutes. Put the sheet pan with the tortillas into the oven at the same time and cook until warmed through, about 4 minutes.

To assemble the tacos, arrange two tortillas on each individual plate. Top each tortilla with cabbage, dividing it evenly, then arrange two or three pieces of fish on each mound of cabbage. Spoon some pico de gallo over the fish, then drizzle about 1 tablespoon of the aioli on top. Serve at once, with the lime wedges and any remaining aioli on the side.

SEARED HALIBUT

WITH CHERRY TOMATO FREGOLA SARDA AND SALSA VERDE

For the salsa verde:

¼ cup extra-virgin olive oil

Leaves from 1 bunch flat-leaf
  parsley, finely chopped

2 small olive oil–packed anchovy
  fillets, chopped

1 tablespoon drained capers, minced

1 small clove garlic, minced

Pinch of red pepper flakes

**For the cherry tomato
  fregola sarda:**

1 tablespoon plus 1 teaspoon
  kosher salt

8 oz fregola sarda or pearl couscous

5 tablespoons extra-virgin olive oil

1 cup small cherry tomatoes, halved
  if large

1 small shallot, thinly sliced

2 cloves garlic, minced

¼ cup dry white wine

4 large fresh basil leaves, thinly sliced

3 tablespoons unsalted butter

¼ cup crumbled ricotta salata cheese

4 skin-on halibut fillets, each
  about 6 oz

Kosher salt and freshly ground
  black pepper

¼ cup canola oil

¼ cup microgreens, for garnish
  (optional)

Makes 4 servings

Halibut, which has a delicate but distinctive taste, easily and gracefully takes on the flavors of the ingredients with which it is paired. Here, it rests on a bed of *fregola sarda*, a small, round Sardinian pasta, that we toss with butter, cherry tomatoes, shallots, garlic, and ricotta salata. Then we top the halibut with a *salsa verde* of parsley, anchovy, capers, and garlic, which adds a complex layer of salt and acid that ties everything together. Make this recipe in summertime, when your garden or the local farmers' market is bursting with sun-ripened tomatoes. The cherry tomato *fregola sarda* is also an excellent accompaniment to any grilled meat or fish and is a great dish to tote along to a potluck or a picnic.

To make the salsa verde, in a small bowl, whisk together the oil, parsley, anchovies, capers, garlic, and pepper flakes. Cover and set aside at room temperature.

To make the fregola sarda, fill a large pot two-thirds full with water, add 1 tablespoon of the salt, and bring to a boil over high heat. Add the fregola sarda and cook, stirring frequently to keep the pasta from sinking and sticking, until al dente, about 13 minutes or according to package directions. Drain into a colander, transfer to a large bowl, and toss with 2 tablespoons of the oil. Set aside to cool to room temperature.

In a large skillet, warm the remaining 3 tablespoons oil over medium-high heat. Add the cherry tomatoes and shallot and cook, stirring occasionally, until the shallot starts to soften, about 2 minutes. Add the garlic and cook, stirring, until fragrant, about 1 minute. Pour in the wine and deglaze the pan, stirring to dislodge any browned bits from the pan bottom. Season with the remaining 1 teaspoon salt and the basil, then add the butter and heat, stirring, until it melts, about 2 minutes. Add the cooled fregola sarda and stir until the fregola is coated with the sauce, about 1 minute. Removed from the heat, scatter the ricotta salata over the top, and toss to mix well. Transfer the contents of the skillet to the large bowl and set aside.

To cook the halibut, preheat the oven to 375°F while the fregola sarda cooks. Pat the fish dry with a paper towel, then season all over with salt and pepper. In a large ovenproof skillet, warm the oil over medium-high heat. When the oil is hot, add the fish, flesh side down, and cook the fish without moving it until golden brown on the underside, about 3 minutes. Turn the fish skin side down and transfer the pan to the oven. Cook until the fish is opaque throughout, about 5 minutes.

To serve, spoon two large spoonfuls of the fregola sarda mixture onto each individual plate. Top each mound with a halibut fillet, then drizzle the fish with 1 tablespoon of the salsa verde. Garnish with microgreens, if using. Pass the remaining salsa verde on the side.

A Rich Fishing History

In the late 1920s, Nick and Frances Kojich and Frances's brothers, Andy and Mike Matkovich, prospered from the bounty they pulled in from the salty waters of Tomales Bay. Fishing played a big role in Nick's life, first as his livelihood and later as enjoyment in his retirement years. In 1931, he decided to give up commercial fishing and open a seafood outpost in what had been a former herring smokehouse. It was where Nick's Cove stands today.

When Prohibition ended in 1933, Nick realized his dream of owning and operating a bar and restaurant. Here he could still be an integral part of the fishing community, serving them a cold beer and a hearty meal at the end of the day and listening to their stories. Nick ran the business much as it is today: a roadside bar and restaurant with guest cottages for weekend warriors traveling up Highway 1.

In 1950, Andrew and Dorothy Matkovich, Frances's nephew and his wife, became partners in Nick's Cove. During their tenure, they hosted shark and stingray derbies, annual clambakes, and other fun events. Oyster farming was already well established in the area, with Tomales Bay Oyster Company having opened in 1909. Today, the roadside along Highway 1 between Point Reyes and Tomales is lined with cars stopping at not only Tomales Bay Oyster Company but also Hog Island Oyster Company, the Marshall Store, Tony's Seafood Restaurant, and, of course, Nick's Cove.

Nick Kojich overseeing the rebuilding of Nick's Cove, circa 1951.

BEER-BATTERED FRIED FISH

WITH HOMEMADE TARTAR SAUCE

For the tartar sauce:
¼ cup drained and roughly
   chopped cornichons
1 tablespoon drained capers
Leaves from 2 fresh dill sprigs
Leaves from 2 fresh tarragon sprigs
4 fresh mint leaves
Juice of ½ lemon
1 teaspoon kosher salt
1½ cups mayonnaise

1½ cups all-purpose flour
3 teaspoons baking soda
¼ teaspoon kosher salt
1½ cups pilsner beer (such as
   Lagunitas pilsner)
3 teaspoons malt vinegar
Canola oil, for deep-frying
1½ lb rock cod fillets, cut into
   6 equal pieces (about 4 oz each)
2 lemons, quartered, for serving

Makes 4 to 6 servings

Close your eyes and imagine sitting outside on our waterfront pier, breathing in the salty coastal air, hearing the sound of the water lapping beneath you, basking in the sunshine warming your face. You take your first bite of beer-battered fried fish topped with a big dollop of our house-made tartar sauce and follow it up with a couple of hand-cut Kennebec fries. At that moment, I'm pretty sure you would agree that there's no better way to spend an afternoon! Our crisp and crunchy batter gets lots of flavor from the local Lagunitas pilsner, and the tartar sauce is laced with fresh herbs from our on-site garden. If possible, use our recipe for Hand-Cut Kennebec Fries (page 59) to accompany the fish. It takes a bit of time, but it is worth every moment. Fry them just before you fry the fish, then you can use the same oil to fry the fish.

To make the tartar sauce, in a food processor, combine the cornichons, capers, dill, tarragon, mint, lemon juice, and salt and process until combined but not liquefied, about 1 minute. Put the mayonnaise into a medium bowl and fold in the cornichon mixture until well mixed. Taste for seasoning and adjust with salt if needed. Cover and refrigerate until ready to use. (The sauce will keep in an airtight container for up to 5 days.)

In a large bowl, whisk together the flour, baking soda, and salt. Add the beer and vinegar and whisk until combined.

Fill a large Dutch oven or other heavy pot half full with oil. Place over high heat and heat until the oil registers 325°F on a deep-fry thermometer. Line a large ovenproof plate with paper towels and place the near the stove. Preheat the oven to 200°F.

When the oil is ready, working in batches of two or three pieces of fish to avoid crowding, dip each piece of the fish into the batter, coating it liberally; lift it out, letting the excess batter drip back into bowl; and then carefully slip it into the hot oil. Cook the fish, turning the pieces once or twice, until crispy golden brown and cooked through, 4 to 6 minutes. Using tongs or a slotted spatula, transfer to the towel-lined plate to drain and place in the oven to keep warm. Repeat with the remaining fish.

Serve the fish at once, accompanied with the tartar sauce and lemons.

GRILLED SALMON

WITH DASHI AND COCONUT STICKY RICE

For the dashi:

1 bunch green onions, white and
　green parts, roughly chopped
1 sheet kombu seaweed, about
　4 by 6 inches
10 dried shiitake mushrooms
¼ cup bonito flakes
¼ cup peeled and chopped
　fresh ginger
4 cloves garlic, peeled
½ cup low-sodium soy sauce

For the coconut sticky rice:

1 cup Thai purple or white sticky rice
2½-inch piece fresh ginger, peeled
　and cut into four ¼-inch-thick slices
1 (13½-oz) can coconut milk, well
　shaken before opening
¼ teaspoon kosher salt

4 salmon fillets, each about 6 oz
　and 1½ inches thick
2 tablespoons extra-virgin olive oil
Kosher salt and freshly ground
　black pepper
Daikon radish sprouts or micro-
　greens, for garnish (optional)

Makes 4 servings

This dramatic dish is bursting with the flavor of the sea. Salmon pairs beautifully with the savory-sweet rice, and the dashi adds depth and flavor. Thai purple sticky rice is higher in antioxidants than white or brown rice and has a naturally sweeter flavor, which is why it is great made with coconut milk. We boil-steam the sticky rice with the coconut milk, which is an unconventional way to prepare it (it is traditionally soaked for a couple of hours and then steamed), but the method yields a wonderful, slightly sticky yet creamy texture that goes perfectly with the salmon. Look for Thai glutinous rice—sometimes labeled "sweet rice"— either purple or white; kombu (dried seaweed); and bonito flakes (flaked dried smoked bonito, a type of tuna) at an Asian market.

To make the dashi, in a medium pot, combine the green onions, kombu, mushrooms, bonito flakes, ginger, garlic, soy sauce, and 6 cups water and bring to a boil over high heat. Boil for about 5 minutes, then reduce the heat to medium and simmer until reduced to about 2 cups, about 30 minutes. Strain the dashi through a fine-mesh sieve, discard the solids, and return the dashi to the saucepan. Cover to keep warm. (The dashi can be cooled and stored in an airtight container in the refrigerator for up to 3 days.)

To make the rice, in a medium saucepan, combine the rice, ginger, coconut milk, salt, and ½ cup water and bring to a boil over high heat. Boil for about 4 minutes, then reduce the heat to medium-low and cook, stirring occasionally, until all the liquid is absorbed and the rice is tender, about 15 minutes. Remove from the heat and discard the ginger slices. Cover the rice to keep warm.

While the dashi and rice are cooking, prepare a charcoal or gas grill for direct cooking over medium-high heat (400°F). Brush the grill grate clean.

Brush the salmon all over with the oil, then season with salt and pepper. Arrange the salmon, skin side up, on the grate and grill, with the lid closed, until nicely grill marked on the underside, about 4 minutes. Turn the salmon over and cook until done to your liking, about 4 minutes longer for medium. Transfer to a cutting board and let rest for 10 minutes.

To serve, divide the rice evenly among four shallow bowls. Top each serving with a salmon fillet, skin side down. Reheat the dashi if it has cooled, then divide it evenly among the bowls, pouring it over the fish and rice. Garnish with the sprouts, if using. Serve at once.

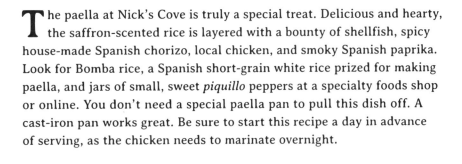

NICK'S COVE PAELLA

1 pound boneless, skinless
  chicken thighs
¼ cup dry sherry
Kosher salt and freshly ground
  black pepper
3 teaspoons smoked paprika
1 cup dry white wine
3 teaspoons saffron threads
1 tablespoon extra-virgin olive oil,
  plus more for drizzling
1 large yellow onion, minced
3 large cloves garlic, minced
2½ cups (1 lb) Bomba rice
¼ cup canola oil
1 lb Spanish chorizo, sliced
25 Manila clams, scrubbed clean
25 medium mussels, scrubbed
  clean and beards removed
12 large Gulf white shrimp in the
  shell, peeled and deveined
6 jarred piquillo peppers, drained
  and thinly sliced
1 cup low-sodium chicken broth
1 bunch green onions, green
  parts only, thinly sliced
2 lemons, cut into wedges,
  for serving

Makes 6 servings

The paella at Nick's Cove is truly a special treat. Delicious and hearty, the saffron-scented rice is layered with a bounty of shellfish, spicy house-made Spanish chorizo, local chicken, and smoky Spanish paprika. Look for Bomba rice, a Spanish short-grain white rice prized for making paella, and jars of small, sweet *piquillo* peppers at a specialty foods shop or online. You don't need a special paella pan to pull this dish off. A cast-iron pan works great. Be sure to start this recipe a day in advance of serving, as the chicken needs to marinate overnight.

In a large zippered plastic bag, combine the chicken, sherry, 1½ teaspoons salt, and 1½ teaspoons of the paprika. Force the air from the bag, seal it closed, and then shake the bag to coat the chicken evenly with the seasonings. Refrigerate overnight.

The next day, prepare a charcoal or gas grill for direct cooking over medium-high heat (400°F), or preheat a stove-top grill pan over medium-high heat. Brush the grill grate clean.

Remove the chicken from the marinade and discard the marinade. Arrange the chicken on the grill grate or stove-top grill pan and grill until golden and nicely grill marked on the first side, about 6 minutes. Turn the chicken over and grill until golden and grill marked on the second side and cooked through, about 5 minutes longer. Transfer to a cutting board and let cool slightly, then cut the chicken into ½-inch-wide strips. Set aside.

In a small bowl, stir together the wine and 1½ teaspoons of the saffron. In a medium bowl, stir together 4 cups water with the remaining 1½ teaspoons saffron. Set aside.

In a large saucepan, warm the 1 tablespoon olive oil over medium heat. Add the yellow onion and cook, stirring occasionally, until softened, about 4 minutes. Add the garlic and cook, stirring, until fragrant, 1 to 2 minutes. Add the rice, 2 teaspoons salt, and 1 teaspoon black pepper and cook, stirring often, until the rice is toasted and fragrant, about 5 minutes. Add the wine-saffron mixture and deglaze the pan, stirring to dislodge any browned bits from the pan bottom. Bring to a boil, stirring occasionally, to cook off the alcohol in the wine, about 3 minutes. Add the saffron-water mixture, 1 cup at a time, cooking and stirring frequently after each addition for 5 minutes, for a total of 20 minutes. When all the liquid has been absorbed and the rice is tender, stir in the remaining 1½ teaspoons paprika. Remove from the heat.

continued . . .

Preheat the oven to 400°F. In a 12-inch paella pan or cast-iron skillet, warm the canola oil over medium-high heat. Add the chorizo and cook, stirring, until slightly crispy, about 6 minutes. Add the clams and mussels, discarding any that fail to close to the touch, along with the reserved chicken, shrimp, and piquillo peppers and cook, stirring occasionally, for about 2 minutes.

Stir in the reserved rice and then add the broth and stir to distribute all the ingredients evenly. Season with salt and pepper, spread the mixture into an even layer, and transfer the pan to the oven. Cook until the rice has crisped up around the pan edges, the shrimp are pink and opaque, the chicken is warmed through, and the clams and mussels have opened, about 6 minutes. Discard any clams or mussels that failed to open.

Drizzle the top of the paella with olive oil and garnish with the green onions. Serve at once, with the lemon wedges on the side.

Main Courses

NICK'S COVE BURGER

WITH SWEET GARLIC AIOLI AND QUICK PICKLES

For the quick pickles:
½ cup white wine vinegar
½ bunch dill, sprigs left whole
1 clove garlic, sliced
1 bay leaf
½ teaspoon red pepper flakes
½ teaspoon yellow mustard seeds
1½ tablespoons kosher salt
1 cup ice cubes
2 pickling cucumbers, cut into
⅛-inch-thick rounds

For the sweet garlic aioli:
½ cup extra-virgin olive oil
3 cloves garlic, unpeeled
2 egg yolks
1 teaspoon fresh lemon juice
½ teaspoon kosher salt

2 lb ground beef
1 tablespoon kosher salt
2 teaspoons freshly ground
  black pepper
4 brioche burger buns, split
½ small red onion, thinly sliced
1 large heirloom tomato, sliced
  about ¼ inch thick (optional)
4 butter lettuce leaves

Makes 4 servings

The trick to making the best burger is to use the best ingredients. We top our patties with thick slices of in-season tomatoes, homegrown lettuce, and house-made garlic aioli and pickles. If tomatoes are not in season, we simply don't use them! We are proud to use grass-fed ground beef from the fourth-generation, family-run Stemple Creek Ranch here in Tomales. Their beef is the best we've tried, but if you don't live nearby, we suggest seeking out freshly ground, grass-fed beef that is locally raised in your community. At the restaurant, this towering burger comes with our popular Hand-Cut Kennebec Fries (page 59).

To make the pickles, in a small saucepan, combine ¾ cup water, the vinegar, dill, garlic, bay leaf, pepper flakes, mustard seeds, and salt over medium-high heat and bring to a simmer, stirring to dissolve the salt. Remove from the heat. Put the ice into a heatproof airtight container and pour the hot brine over the ice. Add the cucumbers to the brine and let cool to room temperature. Refrigerate for at least 24 hours before using. (The pickles will keep in the refrigerator for up to 1 month.)

To make the aioli, in a small saucepan, warm the oil and garlic cloves over low heat; do not allow the mixture to come to a simmer. Cook until the garlic browns and softens, about 20 minutes. Remove from the heat, then transfer the garlic cloves to a plate to cool. Squeeze each clove near its base to release the clove into a medium bowl. Discard the papery sheaths. Let the oil cool to room temperature.

Whisk the egg yolks, lemon juice, and salt into the garlic until combined. While whisking, add the reserved oil in a very slow, thin, steady drizzle. As you beat, the mixture will emulsify; if not, stop adding the oil and whisk vigorously to get a smooth, creamy consistency, then continue adding the oil until a thick sauce forms. Cover and refrigerate until ready to use, up to 4 days in advance.

To make the burgers, prepare a charcoal or gas grill for direct cooking over medium-high heat (400°F). Brush the grill grate clean. In a bowl, combine the ground beef with the salt and pepper and mix until evenly blended. Divide the meat into four equal portions (each 8 oz) and form each portion into a patty about 4 inches in diameter and 1 inch thick. Arrange the patties on the grate and grill until the underside is nicely seared, about 3 minutes. Turn the burgers and cook to your desired doneness, about 3 minutes for medium-rare. Transfer the patties to a plate. Place the buns, cut sides down, on the grate until nicely toasted, about 1 minute.

To assemble the burgers, place the bun bottoms cut side up on individual plates. Top each bottom with a burger. Spread about 1 tablespoon of the aioli on the cut side of each bun top. Top the burgers, in order, with the pickles, onion slices, tomato slices (if using), and butter lettuce. Close the burger with the bun top and serve at once.

ESPRESSO-MARINATED FLAT IRON STEAK

½ cup freshly brewed espresso
or strong coffee
2 shallots, minced
3 cloves garlic, minced
3 tablespoons red wine vinegar
2 tablespoons extra-virgin olive oil
1½ teaspoons kosher salt
1 teaspoon smoked paprika
1 teaspoon freshly ground
black pepper
Two 1-lb flat iron steaks, trimmed
of excess fat and halved crosswise

Makes 4 to 6 servings

Cut with the grain from the shoulder, the flat iron steak can sometimes be a bit tougher than its popular rivals, the rib eye and the New York, but it is also well marbled, which equals great beefy flavor. Impressive yet easy to make, this dish is especially good served with roasted and smashed fingerling potatoes and grilled or roasted asparagus. Be sure to start marinating the steak in the morning or even the night before you plan to cook and serve it.

To marinate the steaks, in a small bowl, whisk together the espresso, shallots, garlic, vinegar, oil, salt, paprika, and pepper. Arrange the steaks in a single layer in a baking dish, pour the marinade evenly over them, and then turn the steaks to coat evenly. Cover the dish and refrigerate, turning the steaks once or twice, for at least 6 hours or up to overnight.

Prepare a charcoal or gas grill for direct heat cooking over high heat (450°F). Brush the grill grate clean.

Remove the steaks from the marinade and pat dry with paper towels. Arrange the steaks on the grate and grill, turning once or twice and with the lid closed as much as possible, until nicely grill marked and done to your liking, about 7 minutes for medium-rare. Transfer to a cutting board and let rest for 5 minutes.

Slice the steak against the grain, arrange on a platter, and serve at once.

DID YOU KNOW?

Don't worry, adding coffee to your marinade won't make your steak taste like coffee—or keep you up all night! Coffee adds a deep earthiness that is slightly bitter, but not overwhelming, and you will see it makes a perfect steak seasoning. Plus, because coffee is acidic, it also tenderizes the meat while it marinates, making it even more delectable.

GRILLED WAGYU STEAK

WITH ROASTED VEGETABLES AND RED WINE SAUCE

For the red wine sauce:

3 cups dry red wine, such as
    cabernet sauvignon or merlot
3 tablespoons packed
    dark brown sugar
½ teaspoon kosher salt
1 bay leaf
1 teaspoon chopped fresh
    thyme leaves

For the roasted vegetables:

1½ lb fingerling or small red
    potatoes, halved lengthwise
1 lb cipollini onions or shallots
3 tablespoons extra-virgin olive oil
1 tablespoon minced garlic
2 teaspoons kosher salt
1 teaspoon freshly ground
    black pepper

For the grilled Wagyu:

2 (1-lb) Wagyu sirloin, flat iron,
    or hanger steaks
1 tablespoon extra-virgin olive oil
2 teaspoons kosher salt
1 teaspoon freshly cracked
    black pepper
Roughly chopped fresh herbs such
    as chives or flat-leaf parsley,
    for garnish (optional)

Makes 4 to 6 servings

In all my years of reading cookbooks and food magazines, testing recipes, and running a restaurant, I've found that it's often the simple recipes that are the most rewarding, and this recipe for grilled Wagyu beef is a good example of that discovery. The consistent marbling of Wagyu beef not only makes this a forgiving protein to work with, but when cooked to medium-rare, it results in a tender and oh-so-juicy steak. The red wine sauce and roasted potatoes and onions elevate this dish to sophisticated.

To make the sauce, in a heavy medium saucepan, combine the wine, sugar, salt, bay leaf, and thyme over low heat and bring to a gentle simmer. Cook, stirring every so often, until reduced by two-thirds, 45 to 60 minutes. Strain through a fine-mesh sieve, discarding the solids, and then return to the saucepan. Cover to keep warm and set aside.

To make the roasted vegetables, preheat the oven to 350°F. In a large bowl, combine the potatoes and onions with the oil, garlic, salt, and pepper and toss to coat evenly. Spread into a single layer on a large sheet pan.

Roast the vegetables, turning once or twice, until nicely browned and tender, about 35 minutes. Cover to keep warm and set aside.

While the vegetables are roasting, prepare a charcoal or gas grill for direct heat cooking over medium heat (350°F). Brush the grill grate clean.

Rub the steaks all over with the oil, then season with salt and pepper. Arrange the steaks on the grate and grill, turning once or twice and with the lid closed as much as possible, until nicely grill marked and done to your liking, about 6 minutes for medium-rare. Transfer to a cutting board and let rest for 10 minutes.

To serve, cut the steaks against the grain into ¼-inch-thick slices. Arrange the roasted vegetables in a bed on a platter and lay the steak slices over the vegetables. Gently reheat the wine sauce and drizzle over the steak, then garnish with the herbs, if using. Serve at once.

The Cottages

All the cottages at Nick's Cove were created out of original structures that existed when the property was owned by Nick and Frances Kojich in the 1920s. Rich in history, each cottage was given a meaningful name—as well as upgraded—when Nick's was reopened in 2007. Some of the names are more personal than others, but all of them have a great story.

The cottages called Al's and Ruthie's were named after Al and Ruth Gibson, who owned and operated the property from the mid-1970s to the late 1990s. Bandit's and Joker's Shed were originally located on the west side of Tomales Bay in an encampment. After Nick purchased the land, he moved the structures across the bay on a barge and placed them in the same spot where they stand today. These two cottages were named for *Bandits*, a movie starring Bruce Willis, Billy Bob Thornton, and Cate Blanchett that was filmed at Nick's Cove and released in 2001.

While Nicolina was once a barge on which hay was ferried across the bay, it had been a houseboat on the west side of Tomales Bay before it made its way across to Nick's Cove. It was renovated to include a modest soaking tub and a tiny (but highly efficient) woodburning stove, and today it is our most requested room. It was named after Frances's brother Gregory's wife, Nicolina. Big Rock and Little Rock are so-called for the two rocks that can be seen from inside the cottage at low tide.

Three groups of cottages stand across Highway 1. The red building contains Red Legged Frog, in honor of the local frogs whose habitat we've preserved along the creek; Heart's Desire, which is the lovely protected beach on the west side of the bay near Inverness; and Innkeeper, named for the cottage in which the original innkeeper lived. All three of these cottages were made from what was once a barn. The middle grouping of cottages contains Fly Fisherman, for the many fishermen who came through Nick's Cove over the years, and Uncle Andy's, named after Frances's nephew Andrew (Nicolina's son). Andrew married Dorothy, and in 1950, they became partners with Nick and Frances, a relationship that lasted until the mid-1970s. Andrew and Dorothy had a daughter, Judi, which brings us to the next set of cottages, Judi's and Jerry's. Jerry was Ruth's son and lived in a former iteration of Jerry's cottage.

Nicolina being outfitted to become a cottage, circa 1928.

BRINED PORK CHOPS

WITH APPLE-CORIANDER GLAZE AND BRAISED CABBAGE

For the apple brine:
3 cups cider vinegar
3 cups apple juice
½ cup kosher salt
¼ cup packed light brown sugar
8 black peppercorns
2 shallots, roughly chopped
4 fresh rosemary sprigs
2 cloves garlic, chopped
1 lemon, quartered
4 cups ice cubes

4 bone-in, center-cut pork loin chops,
  each about 8 oz and 1 inch thick

For the apple-coriander glaze:
2 cups apple juice
2 tablespoons coriander seeds
1 teaspoon kosher salt
1 bay leaf

For the braised cabbage:
3 tablespoons extra-virgin olive oil
1 small red onion, thinly sliced
1 small head red cabbage, quartered
  lengthwise, cored, and sliced
  crosswise ¼ inch thick
1 cup dry white wine
1 cup apple cider vinegar
1 tablespoon caraway seeds
¼ cup sugar
2 teaspoons kosher salt

Makes 4 servings

The first time you tried brined pork, you probably, like most people, immediately recognized how different it tasted from regular pork: juicier and more tender and flavorful. This recipe is proof of all that and more. The glaze that dresses the brined chops combines the sweetness of apple with the nutty citrus of coriander, complementing not only the pork but also the side of braised cabbage. Together, the pork chops and cabbage are a stellar example of a hearty and satisfying meal. For the tastiest results, brine the pork overnight.

To make the brine, in a medium pot, combine the vinegar, apple juice, salt, sugar, peppercorns, shallots, rosemary, garlic, and lemon, place over high heat, and bring to a rapid boil, stirring to dissolve the salt and sugar, about 12 minutes. Remove from the heat and add the ice. Set aside to cool completely. Once the brine is cold, add the pork chops. Cover and refrigerate for at least 3 hours or up to overnight.

For the apple-coriander glaze, in a medium saucepan, whisk together the apple juice, coriander, salt, and bay leaf and bring to a boil over medium-high heat. Reduce the heat to medium-low and boil gently until the mixture is reduced by three-fourths and is syrupy, about 20 minutes. Strain through a fine-mesh sieve into a heatproof bowl. Set aside at room temperature until ready to use.

For the cabbage, in a heavy medium pot, warm the oil over medium-high heat. Add the onion and cook, stirring, until starting to sweat, about 2 minutes. Add the cabbage and toss to combine. Cook, stirring occasionally, until the cabbage softens, about 3 minutes. Add the wine and vinegar, stirring to dislodge any browned bits, then stir in the caraway seeds. Reduce the heat to medium, and cook, stirring occasionally, until the cabbage is tender, about 10 minutes. Add the sugar and salt and stir to mix well. Continue to cook, stirring occasionally, until barely any liquid is left in the pot, 10 to 15 minutes. Set aside and cover to keep warm.

Remove the chops from the brine, pat dry with paper towels, and let rest at room temperature for 15 minutes before grilling. Discard the brine.

Prepare a charcoal or gas grill for direct heat cooking over medium-high heat (400°F). Brush the grill grate clean. Arrange the chops on the grate and grill, turning once or twice and with the lid closed as much as possible, until nicely grill marked and an instant-read thermometer inserted into the center of a chop registers 140°F, about 10 minutes. They should be cooked to medium, or slightly pink in the middle. Transfer to a plate and let rest for 5 minutes.

Divide the cabbage evenly among four individual plates and top each serving with a pork chop. Drizzle the chops with the apple-coriander glaze and serve at once.

GOAT MEATBALLS

WITH SPICY TOMATO-LEEK SAUCE

For the meatballs:

2 lb ground goat or lamb

1 small carrot, peeled and minced

1 small white onion, minced

1 celery stalk, minced

2 cloves garlic, minced

1 tablespoon chopped fresh
flat-leaf parsley

2 teaspoons kosher salt

1 teaspoon freshly ground
black pepper

For the tomato-leek sauce:

2 tablespoons extra-virgin olive oil

5 medium leeks, white parts only,
halved lengthwise and sliced
crosswise ¼ inch thick

¼ cup dry white wine

3 (16-oz) cans crushed tomatoes
with juice

1 tablespoon balsamic vinegar

2 teaspoons ground fennel

1 teaspoon red pepper flakes

Kosher salt and freshly ground
black pepper

¼ cup plus 1 tablespoon
extra-virgin olive oil

½ cup fresh bread crumbs

½ cup grated Parmesan cheese

Makes 4 servings

We are proud to serve goat meat from Rossotti Ranch, a true ranch-to-table producer out here in West Marin. The goats are raised and harvested humanely, and their meat has a deliciously robust flavor that is perfect for making our meatballs, which we braise in a house-made tomato-leek sauce. What we love most about these meatballs is their versatility. They are great with spaghetti, in a sandwich, or, our favorite way, with some French bread and a green salad. If goat is not readily available, lamb is a good substitute, as it lends a similar depth of flavor—a quality you just don't find with beef.

Preheat the oven to 450°F. Line a large sheet pan with parchment paper.

To make the meatballs, in a large bowl, combine the goat, carrot, onion, celery, garlic, parsley, salt, and pepper and, using your hands, mix until well blended. For each meatball, scoop up about ¼ cup of the meat mixture, gently shape it into a ball, and place on the prepared pan.

Roast the meatballs until the outsides are nicely browned, about 10 minutes. Remove from the oven and set aside. Reduce the oven temperature to 375°F.

To make the sauce, in a large, heavy pot, warm the oil over medium-low heat. Add the leeks and cook, stirring occasionally, until tender, about 10 minutes. Pour in the wine and deglaze the pot, stirring to scrape up any browned bits from the pot bottom. Add the tomatoes and their juice, the vinegar, fennel, and pepper flakes and season with salt and pepper. Increase the heat to medium and cook, stirring occasionally, until reduced by about half, about 20 minutes.

Transfer the meatballs to a large baking dish, arranging them in a single layer. Pour the sauce over the meatballs and cover the dish with aluminum foil or a lid. Bake until the meatballs are cooked through and the sauce is bubbling, 15 to 20 minutes.

While the meatballs are baking, toast the bread crumbs. In a dry small skillet, warm 1 tablespoon of the oil over medium heat. Add the bread crumbs and cook, stirring, until golden brown, about 4 minutes.

When the meatballs are ready, remove from the oven and drizzle with the remaining ¼ cup oil, sprinkle with the toasted bread crumbs, and finish with the Parmesan cheese. Serve at once.

SEARED DUCK BREASTS

WITH CRUNCHY CAULIFLOWER AND HUCKLEBERRY SAUCE

For the berry sauce:
1½ teaspoons extra-virgin olive oil
1 large shallot, roughly chopped
½ cup dry, full-bodied red wine
  (such as cabernet sauvignon)
1 bay leaf
5 black peppercorns
1 tablespoon sugar
1 teaspoon kosher salt
1 lb fresh or frozen Mendocino
  huckleberries or fresh blackberries
  (blackberries quartered if large)

For the cauliflower:
6 tablespoons unsalted butter
1 head cauliflower, trimmed and
  cut into 1-inch florets
1 small yellow onion, minced
Kosher salt and freshly ground
  black pepper
¼ cup fresh bread crumbs

4 boneless, skin-on duck breasts,
  each about 8 oz

Makes 4 servings

Sonoma County Poultry is our local duck farmer and home to the widely praised Liberty Duck. Located just outside the city limits of Petaluma, this boutique business raises ducks naturally, producing what we believe is the best, most flavorful duck in the entire country. If you've never tried to cook duck, this recipe is not only approachable but also yields amazing results. While our restaurant is too big to handpick the berries for the sauce, I highly recommend that, after a satisfying lunch at Nick's Cove, you pull off the road on your way home and pick some blackberries, which grow in profusion along Highway 1.

To make the sauce, in a small saucepan, warm the oil over medium heat. Add the shallot and cook, stirring, until it softens, about 2 minutes. Add the wine, stirring to dislodge any browned bits, then stir in the bay leaf, peppercorns, sugar, salt, and berries. Bring to a simmer, reduce the heat to low, and cook, stirring occasionally, until reduced to a thin syrup, about 30 minutes. Remove from the heat.

Strain the sauce through a fine-mesh sieve into a heatproof small bowl. Discard the solids, or, if you like, discard the bay leaf and peppercorns from the solids in the sieve, then reserve ½ cup of the solids in a separate small bowl. Return the strained sauce to the saucepan and set aside.

To make the cauliflower, preheat the oven to 350°F. Melt 4 tablespoons of the butter. Add the cauliflower and onion to an 8-inch square baking dish and drizzle with the melted butter. Season with salt and pepper and toss to combine. In a small skillet over medium heat, melt the remaining 2 tablespoons butter. Add the bread crumbs and cook, stirring, until toasted, about 2 minutes. Scatter the bread crumbs evenly over the top of the cauliflower mixture, then season with salt and pepper. Bake until the cauliflower is tender and the bread crumbs are golden brown, about 30 minutes. Keep warm.

While the cauliflower is baking, prepare the duck. Using a sharp knife, make five diagonal slits, about ½ inch apart and as long as the skin, through the skin and fat of each breast, being careful not to cut into the meat. Place the duck breasts, skin side down, into a cold large, heavy skillet. Turn on the heat to medium. Cook until the fat browns, about 10 minutes. Turn the duck breasts over and cook meat side down for 10 minutes for medium-rare.

Transfer the duck to a cutting board and let rest 5 minutes. Gently rewarm the berry sauce. Divide the warm cauliflower among four plates. Slice each breast on the diagonal and place on top of the cauliflower. Drizzle with the warm sauce. Garnish with the reserved berries, if you reserved them. Serve at once.

ROAST CHICKEN

WITH BUTTERY PAN JUICES

For the brine:
6 cups orange juice
⅓ cup kosher salt
½ bunch thyme
8 whole cardamom pods, or
  1 teaspoon ground cardamom
2 tablespoons coriander seeds,
  or 1 tablespoon ground coriander
2 bay leaves
1 teaspoon red pepper flakes
4 cups ice
1 whole chicken, 3 to 4 lb

¼ cup extra-virgin olive oil
½ cup dry white wine
1 cup low-sodium chicken broth
3 tablespoons unsalted butter,
  cut into pieces

Makes 4 servings

There's nothing homier than a richly browned, crisp-skinned roast chicken. This is the recipe that I like to serve for a special dinner with old friends, and it is especially good with our Savory Mushroom Bread Pudding (page 135) and a pile of Garlicky Greens (facing page). Be sure to start this recipe a day or two in advance so the chicken is brined long enough, as that important step keeps the meat juicy and imbues it with lovely flavor.

Select a pot large enough to hold the brine and the chicken. Add 2 cups water, the orange juice, salt, thyme, cardamom, coriander, bay leaves, and pepper flakes to the pot and place over medium heat. Bring to a simmer, stirring until the salt dissolves. Remove from the heat, add the ice, and let cool completely.

Add the chicken to the cooled brine, cover, and refrigerate for at least 8 hours or up to 48 hours.

Preheat the oven to 350°F. Remove the chicken from the brine and discard the brine. Rinse the chicken under cold running water and then pat dry with paper towels. Place the chicken, breast side up, in a roasting pan or large ovenproof skillet. Tie the legs together with kitchen twine. Rub the chicken all over with the olive oil.

If you are making the bread pudding to accompany the chicken as suggested in the headnote, bake it alongside the chicken.

Roast the chicken for 50 minutes, then baste the chicken with the pan juices. Continue to roast the chicken until it is crisp and golden brown and an instant-read thermometer inserted into the thickest part of the thigh away from bone registers 160°F, 15 to 20 minutes longer. Transfer the chicken to a cutting board and let rest for about 10 minutes while you make the buttery pan juices.

If you are making the greens to accompany the chicken as suggested in the head-note, prepare them while you make the buttery pan juices.

Discard any excess oil from the roasting pan or skillet and place over medium-high heat. Add the wine and deglaze the pan, stirring to dislodge any browned bits from the pan bottom. Simmer for 1 minute. Add the chicken broth and butter, and continue to simmer, stirring frequently, until the mixture is reduced by half and a sauce forms, about 5 minutes. Remove from the heat.

To carve the chicken, holding it steady with a large fork, and using a sharp carving knife, cut through the skin between the leg and body, then continue through the hip joint, removing the leg from the body. Remove the other leg the same way. Place the leg skin side down and cut through the joint, separating the drumstick and thigh. Repeat with the second leg. To carve the breast meat, make a deep, horizontal cut at the base of each breast toward the bone. Then cut vertically between the two breasts and remove each breast from the breastbone. Carve the breast meat into slices. Bend a wing away from the body and cut through the shoulder joint to remove the wing. Repeat with the other wing.

To assemble the dish, if you have also made the bread pudding and the greens, spoon the greens in an even layer onto a large serving platter. Place the squares of bread pudding around the greens. Arrange the chicken pieces on top of the greens and drizzle with the buttery pan juices. If you have not made the two side dishes, arrange the chicken pieces on a large platter and drizzle the buttery pan juices over the top. Serve at once.

GARLICKY GREENS

2 tablespoons extra-virgin olive oil
1 tablespoon unsalted butter
1 bunch Swiss chard, stems and ribs
 removed and leaves cut into
 ½-inch-wide ribbons
2 large cloves garlic, minced
2 tablespoons dry white wine
½ teaspoon freshly ground
 black pepper
Kosher salt

Makes 4 servings

In a large skillet, warm the oil and butter over medium-high heat. Add the chard and garlic and cook, stirring, until the chard starts to wilt, about 1 minute. Pour in the wine and deglaze the pan, stirring to dislodge any browned bits from the pan bottom. Add the pepper and cook, stirring, until most of the liquid has evaporated, about 2 minutes. Season to taste with salt.

Serve at once, or cover and keep warm until ready to serve.

SAVORY MUSHROOM BREAD PUDDING

1 (12-oz) sourdough baguette or
  batard, cut into 1-inch cubes

3 tablespoons extra-virgin olive oil

12 oz cremini mushrooms, cleaned,
  stem ends trimmed, and finely
  chopped

1 large shallot, minced

1 cup dry white wine

1 tablespoon minced fresh thyme

3 large eggs

1½ cups whole milk

1½ cups heavy cream

2 teaspoons kosher salt

Makes 4 servings

C hef Kua Speer's savory bread pudding blends the earthy flavors of mushrooms and thyme to create a perfectly moist, crisp-topped side dish. While it is a great accompaniment to our roast chicken, it is also a satisfying vegetarian main course, served with a lightly dressed green salad. If you enjoy foraging for mushrooms or want to try the mushrooms available at your local farmers' market, feel free to substitute other fungi for the cremini.

Preheat the oven to 350°F. Generously oil a 9-inch square baking pan with olive oil.

Put the bread cubes into a large bowl. In a large skillet, warm the oil over medium-high heat. Add the mushrooms and cook, stirring occasionally, until the mushrooms start to soften, 4 to 5 minutes. Add the shallot and cook, stirring occasionally, until the shallot starts to soften, about 3 minutes. Pour in the wine and deglaze the pan, stirring to dislodge any browned bits from the pan bottom. Add the thyme and cook, stirring occasionally, until the liquid is reduced by half, about 2 minutes. Transfer the contents of the skillet to the bowl with the bread cubes and toss until all the ingredients are evenly distributed.

In a medium bowl, whisk the eggs until blended, then whisk in the milk, cream, and salt until fully incorporated. Add the egg mixture to the bread mixture and toss to mix evenly. Let stand for 5 minutes.

Transfer the egg-bread mixture to the prepared pan and press it down firmly into the pan. Bake until the top is crispy and golden brown, about 35 minutes. Transfer to a wire rack and let cool for 15 minutes.

Cut the pudding into four squares and serve warm.

WEST MARIN FARMING

West Marin has long been a farming community, with generations of immigrant families calling the area home. The richness of the soil, the mild coastal climate, and the proximity to the bay drew the earliest settlers, who quickly created communities in which they raised families rich in the culture of their homeland.

Historically, this rural region has seen many types of farming, but it is most widely known for its dairies, with the first dairymen settling here in the mid-1800s. They came from Ireland, Portugal, and Switzerland, and established small farms where they milked their herd by hand.

Tomales was a busy shipping port in those days, and much of what the dairies produced was sent out on schooners to San Francisco. The influence of these early farmers can still be seen as you wind your way along Highway 1 past dairy farms and creameries, many of them run by descendants of the immigrant families whose dedication and tireless work helped establish this farming paradise.

Thanks to the Point Reyes National Seashore and the Marin Agricultural Land Trust, this farming tradition will stay protected into the future. One of the stars of this thriving rural community is Straus Family Creamery, which sits adjacent to Nick's Cove. Straus, which was founded in 1941, was the first dairy west of the Mississippi to become certified organic and the first creamery to become certified organic in the United States. We are honored to call West Marin home and love being a place where our talented, innovative, and friendly farming neighbors come in, sit at the bar, and enjoy one another's company.

West Marin dairy cows grazing in the fields along Tomales Bay.

RABBIT SUGO PAPPARDELLE

For the rabbit sugo:

1 rabbit (2 to 3 lb), quartered

2 teaspoons kosher salt

1 teaspoon freshly ground
  black pepper

3 tablespoons extra-virgin olive oil

1 large yellow onion, finely chopped

4 celery stalks, finely chopped

1 fennel bulb, trimmed, cored,
  and sliced lengthwise into
  ¼-inch-thick pieces

2 bay leaves

2 fresh thyme sprigs

1 cup dry white wine

3 cups low-sodium chicken broth

1 lb fresh pappardelle, or
  12 oz dried pappardelle

2 tablespoons kosher salt

½ cup shredded Parmesan cheese

Leaves from ½ bunch flat-leaf
  parsley, minced

Makes 4 servings

Our version of rabbit *sugo* calls for slowly braising rabbit with fennel, fresh herbs, and plenty of white wine. The result is a silky sauce perfect for topping fresh pasta, especially hand-cut pappardelle. What makes our version extra special is the locally raised rabbits we get from Devil's Gulch Ranch, just up the road in Nicasio. Whenever we can, we strive to use local ingredients that are sourced from within twenty miles of the restaurant. This is a particularly beautiful example of that philosophy.

Preheat the oven to 350°F.

Pat the rabbit pieces dry with paper towels and sprinkle all over with the salt and pepper. In a large, wide Dutch oven or other ovenproof pot, warm the oil over medium-high heat. Add the rabbit and sear, turning and rotating as needed, until the meat is golden brown all over, about 3 minutes on each side. Transfer to a plate and set aside.

Reduce the heat to medium-low, add the onion, celery, and fennel, and cook, stirring occasionally, until the vegetables begin to brown, 5 to 7 minutes. Add the bay leaves, thyme, and wine and deglaze the pot, stirring to dislodge any browned bits from the pot bottom. Cook for 2 minutes. Return the rabbit to the pot, pour in the broth, and then add water as needed to cover the rabbit (about 2 cups). Raise the heat to medium-high and bring the mixture to a simmer, then cover with a tight-fitting lid and transfer to the oven. Cook until the rabbit begins to shred and fall off the bone, about 2 hours.

Carefully transfer the rabbit to a cutting board. Place the pot with the cooking liquid on the stove top over medium heat and simmer, uncovered, for about 15 minutes to reduce the liquid. Once the rabbit is cool enough to handle, pull the meat from the bones and shred the meat with two forks; discard the bones. Add the shredded rabbit meat to the cooking liquid, cover, and remove from the heat.

To cook the pappardelle, fill a large pot two-thirds full with water and bring to a boil over medium-high heat. Add the salt and then the pasta, stir, and cook, stirring occasionally, until al dente, about 3 minutes for fresh pasta, about 7 minutes for dried pasta, or according to package directions. Ladle out 1 cup of the pasta cooking water and set it aside, then drain the pasta and add it to the rabbit sugo. Toss and stir to mix the pasta with the sugo, adding spoonfuls of the pasta water until the desired sauciness is reached.

Divide the mixture among four individual shallow bowls. Garnish each serving with the Parmesan and parsley, dividing them evenly. Serve at once.

ROASTED STUFFED QUAIL

WITH BRIOCHE, CRANBERRIES, AND HERBS

1 loaf brioche, about 14 oz, cut into ½-inch cubes (about 2 cups)

4 tablespoons extra-virgin olive oil

½ cup dried cranberries, roughly chopped

2 celery stalks, finely chopped

1 large shallot, finely chopped

1 clove garlic, finely chopped

4 fresh sage leaves, finely chopped

1 teaspoon finely chopped fresh thyme leaves

½ cup low-sodium chicken broth

1 large egg, lightly beaten

1½ teaspoons kosher salt

8 quail, cleaned

½ teaspoon freshly ground black pepper

Makes 8 servings

Roasting whole stuffed quail might sound overly ambitious, but this elegant recipe couldn't be simpler. Perfectly sized, tender, lean quail is a delightful alternative to chicken or other game fowl. It comes with some big upsides: you don't have to worry about slicing and serving it as you would a whole chicken—your guests do it themselves—and the cooking time is a fraction of that of a whole chicken, which makes it a simple weeknight dinner party option that is quick yet impressive. Quail can be found at well-stocked markets in the butcher department. A favorite of our guests, this dish is terrific with roasted vegetables, such as carrots, fingerling potatoes, or warm cauliflower salad (page 70).

Preheat the oven to 450°F. Spread the brioche in an even layer on a large sheet pan. Bake, stirring once halfway through baking, until the cubes are dried but not browned, 8 to 10 minutes. Set aside to cool.

Meanwhile, in a medium skillet, warm 2 tablespoons of the oil over medium-high heat. Add the dried cranberries, celery, shallot, garlic, sage, and thyme and cook, stirring occasionally, until tender, about 6 minutes. Transfer to a large bowl and let cool for 10 minutes.

Add the brioche cubes and broth to the cooled vegetable mixture and toss and stir to mix well. Add the egg and 1 teaspoon of the salt and mix gently.

Season the outside of the quail evenly with the remaining ½ teaspoon salt and the pepper. Carefully spoon about ¼ cup of the brioche stuffing into the cavity of each quail. Cross the ends of each quail's legs, then tie together with kitchen twine.

In a large skillet, warm the remaining 2 tablespoons oil over medium-high heat. Working in batches to avoid overcrowding, add the quail to the skillet and sear, turning as needed, until the skin is browned on all sides. Transfer the quail to a sheet pan.

Roast the quail until an instant-read thermometer inserted into the thickest part of the quail away from bone registers 160°F, about 15 minutes. Remove from the oven, snip and remove the twine, and transfer to individual plates. Serve at once.

ROAST FENNEL RISOTTO
WITH NASTURTIUM PESTO AND PARMESAN

For the Parmesan stock:
1 (4-oz) piece Parmesan rind
1 small white onion, roughly chopped
1 bay leaf

For the nasturtium pesto:
2 cups packed nasturtium leaves
    or sorrel leaves
¾ cup extra-virgin olive oil
Juice of 1 lemon
3 tablespoons grated Parmesan
    cheese
1 small clove garlic, minced
½ teaspoon kosher salt

For the fennel risotto:
1 large fennel bulb, about 12 oz,
    trimmed, fronds reserved for
    garnish
2 tablespoons extra-virgin olive oil
Kosher salt
2 tablespoons unsalted butter
1½ cups Carnaroli or Arborio rice
¼ cup grated Parmesan cheese

2 teaspoons fennel pollen
4 pesticide-free nasturtium flowers,
    for garnish (optional)

Makes 4 servings

We often have a risotto recipe on the menu. It makes a great vegetarian main course and really warms you up when the fog rolls in. So when we were compiling the recipes for this cookbook, I wanted to make sure a risotto was included. This variation by chef Kua Speer is creamy and warming. Roasting our Croft-grown fennel delivers a wonderful sweetness to the risotto, while the Parmesan stock adds richness and the pesto contributes freshness and color. Look for the fennel pollen, which imparts sweet, floral, anise-like notes, in small bottles at Italian markets or online.

To make the stock, in a medium saucepan, combine the Parmesan rind, onion, bay leaf, and 6 cups water and bring to a simmer over medium-high heat. Cover, remove from the heat, and set aside to steep for 2 hours. Strain the stock through a fine-mesh sieve. If using the stock right away, return it to the saucepan. If not using it right away, store it in an airtight container in the refrigerator for up to 5 days or in the freezer for up to 1 month.

To make the pesto, in a blender, combine the nasturtium leaves, oil, lemon juice, Parmesan cheese, garlic, and salt and blend on medium-high speed until smooth. Set aside at room temperature. (The pesto will keep in an airtight container in the refrigerator for up to 4 days; stir well before using.)

To roast the fennel, preheat the oven to 350°F. Split the fennel bulb in half lengthwise. Place the halves cut side down on a cutting board and cut lengthwise into ¼-inch-thick slices. On a large sheet pan, toss the fennel with the oil, coating evenly, and season with salt. Spread the fennel in a single layer and roast until tender, about 10 minutes. Remove from the oven and set aside.

Bring the stock to a bare simmer over medium-low heat. In a large, wide saucepan, melt the butter over medium heat. Add the rice and cook, stirring continuously, until lightly toasted and fragrant, about 3 minutes. Add a ladleful of the hot stock to the rice, reduce the heat to low, and cook, stirring occasionally so the rice does not stick, until the liquid is absorbed, about 5 minutes. Continue adding the stock, a ladleful at a time, stirring after each addition until nearly fully absorbed before adding more, until all of the stock has been added and been absorbed by the rice. This should take about 30 minutes.

Add the roasted fennel and ½ teaspoon salt and stir to combine. The rice should be tender and moist. If the rice is still firm, add ½ cup hot water and stir over medium heat for about 2 minutes. Remove from the heat and stir in the cheese.

Divide the risotto evenly among four bowls. Garnish each serving with 2 tablespoons pesto, ½ teaspoon fennel pollen, fennel fronds, and a flower (if using). Serve.

HUCKLEBERRY AND GRAVENSTEIN APPLE CRISP

For the topping:

½ cup steel-cut oats

¼ cup packed light brown sugar

2 tablespoons all-purpose flour

1 teaspoon salt

4 tablespoons cold unsalted
butter, diced

¼ cup chopped toasted
walnuts (optional)

3 lb Gravenstein or Granny
Smith apples

3 tablespoons unsalted butter

1 teaspoon pure vanilla extract

1 cup fresh or thawed frozen
Mendocino huckleberries or
fresh blueberries

4 tablespoons granulated sugar,
plus more if needed

Vanilla ice cream, for serving

Makes 4 servings

First planted in Sonoma County in the early nineteenth century, perhaps by fur trappers at the Russian settlement of Fort Ross, the Gravenstein apple had become a valuable local crop by the 1880s. Today, the Gravenstein remains an important symbol of the county's long agricultural history. Greenish yellow with broad red and orange stripes, it ripens in late July, making it one of the first apples in North America ready for market. Crisp and juicy and full of old-fashioned sweet-tart flavor, it is prized for both baking and for eating out of hand.

Preheat the oven to 350°F. To make the topping, in a medium bowl, combine the oats, brown sugar, flour, and salt and stir to mix. Scatter the butter over the top, then, using your fingers, mix in the butter until the mixture is crumbly. Stir in the walnuts (if using), cover, and refrigerate for 20 minutes.

Meanwhile, peel and core the apples, then cut into ¼-inch-thick slices.

In a large skillet, melt the butter over medium heat. Add the apples and vanilla and cook, stirring occasionally, until the apples start to soften, about 4 minutes. Transfer the apples to a large bowl. Add the berries and granulated sugar and toss to combine, adding a little more sugar if the fruit is particularly tart. Transfer to an 8-inch square baking dish.

Sprinkle the chilled oat mixture in an even layer on top of the apple mixture. Bake until the apples are tender, the fruit is bubbling, and the topping is golden brown, about 30 minutes. Let cool on a wire rack for 20 minutes. Serve warm, with scoops of ice cream.

DESSERT PAIRING

Serving dessert with wine takes the experience to the next level. I love to serve this crisp alongside a vibrant glass of Blandy's Madeira Verdelho 1968, which perfectly complements the crisp's sweet apples and tart huckleberries. Other excellent options, which are great for fruit-based desserts such as this, include fizzy Italian Moscato d'Asti or a caramelly Tawny Port.

HOMEMADE S'MORES

For the marshmallows:
1½ tablespoons powdered gelatin
½ cup light corn syrup
1 cup granulated sugar
¼ teaspoon kosher salt
1½ teaspoons vanilla bean paste
  or pure vanilla extract
¼ cup powdered sugar
¼ cup cornstarch

For the graham crackers:
1 cup whole-wheat flour
¼ cup all-purpose flour
½ teaspoon ground cinnamon
¼ teaspoon baking soda
¼ teaspoon kosher salt
⅛ teaspoon freshly grated nutmeg
½ cup unsalted butter, at room
  temperature
⅓ cup granulated sugar
¼ cup honey
½ teaspoon pure vanilla extract

8 squares semisweet or milk
  chocolate (about 4 oz)

Makes 8 s'mores; 4 servings

I grew up camping with my aunt and uncle, and when we made s'mores, there was always a contest to see whose marshmallow ended up perfectly creamy in the center without either burning the outside or dropping the molten goodness into the fire. At Nick's, we wanted to re-create that nostalgic feeling that many associate with experiences they've had around a campfire on Tomales Bay, so we decided to celebrate those special memories with a handcrafted s'mores kit. It comes complete with homemade graham crackers and marshmallows and locally made TCHO chocolate. The best part of this story is that we donate money from every s'mores kit we sell to organizations that help kids in the nearby city of Petaluma. So the box is both *filled* with good things and *does* good things!

To make the marshmallows, in a bowl, whisk together ½ cup lukewarm water with the gelatin. Set aside. In a heavy medium saucepan, whisk together ½ cup water, the corn syrup, granulated sugar, and salt over medium-high heat and bring to a boil, whisking constantly. Clip a candy thermometer onto the side of the pan and cook, stirring occasionally, until the mixture registers 248°F on the thermometer, 10 to 12 minutes. Remove from the heat and allow the syrup to cool to 212°F.

Pour the hot sugar syrup into a stand mixer fitted with the whisk attachment. With the mixer on medium speed, slowly pour the gelatin mixture into the sugar syrup in a thin, steady stream. Add the vanilla bean paste. Continue to beat until light and fluffy, about 10 minutes.

Meanwhile, grease the bottom and sides of a 6-inch square baking dish with melted butter. Sift the powdered sugar and cornstarch together into a bowl, then add ¼ cup of the mixture to the prepared baking dish. Shake and tip the dish until the bottom and sides are evenly coated with the cornstarch mixture.

Using a rubber spatula, scrape the marshmallow mixture into the prepared baking dish and spread in an even layer. Sift 2 tablespoons of the remaining cornstarch mixture evenly over the top of the marshmallow mixture. Cover the dish with plastic wrap and leave at room temperature for at least 8 hours or up to overnight to set. Set the remaining cornstarch mixture aside.

Cut the marshmallows into 1½-inch squares; you should have eight marshmallows. Roll each marshmallow in the remaining cornstarch mixture to coat. Arrange the marshmallows in an airtight container large enough to accommodate them in a single layer without touching. Set aside at room temperature until ready to serve or up to 2 days.

continued . . .

To make the graham crackers, in a medium bowl, whisk together both flours, the cinnamon, baking soda, salt, and nutmeg. In the stand mixer fitted with the paddle attachment, beat together the butter and granulated sugar on medium speed until light and fluffy, about 3 minutes. Add the honey and vanilla and beat until blended, about 1 minute. With the mixer still on medium speed, add the flour mixture in three equal batches, beating well and scraping down the sides of the bowl after each addition. Transfer the dough to a work surface, press into a disk, and let rest for 15 minutes. Meanwhile, preheat the oven to 325°F.

Dust a large piece of parchment paper (about 12 inches square) and a rolling pin with all-purpose flour, then transfer the dough disk to the floured parchment. Roll out the dough into a 10-inch square about ⅛ inch thick. Using a ruler and a pizza wheel or pastry cutter, cut the dough into 2½-inch squares, trimming the edges if needed to even them. Just cut the squares; don't separate them. You should have sixteen squares. Using the tines of a fork, dock each square two or three times. Transfer the parchment with the dough to a large sheet pan.

Bake the squares, rotating the pan back to front once halfway through baking, until golden brown, about 10 minutes. Remove from the oven and, using a small, sharp knife or a metal bench scraper, recut the squares while they are still warm. Let cool completely on the pan on a wire rack, then separate the squares. (The graham crackers will keep in an airtight container at room temperature for up to 6 days.)

To assemble the s'mores, arrange the graham crackers, marshmallows, and chocolate squares on a platter along with some long sticks or roasting skewers. Roast the marshmallows over a fire, then assemble the s'mores by layering a graham cracker with some chocolate, a molten marshmallow, and another graham cracker. Eat right away!

SPICED GINGER CAKE

WITH SANTA ROSA PLUMS

2½ cups all-purpose flour

1 teaspoon ground cinnamon

½ teaspoon ground cloves

½ teaspoon freshly ground
   black pepper

½ teaspoon kosher salt

1 cup molasses (not blackstrap)

1 cup plus 2 tablespoons sugar

1 cup canola oil

¼ cup peeled and grated
   fresh ginger

2 teaspoons baking soda

2 large eggs, at room temperature

6 ripe Santa Rosa or other
   flavorful plums

Makes 6 servings

We like this cake served without any embellishment alongside coffee for breakfast or as a snack anytime throughout the day. But if you want to take it into dessert territory, a dollop of lightly sweetened whipped cream or even whipped crème fraîche is a welcome addition. We use Santa Rosa plums because they are juicy, sweet, and deeply flavored, but you can substitute any ripe plum that tastes good. This recipe, which was created by pastry chef Gillian Helquist, is also great made with sliced peaches, nectarines, or apricots.

Preheat the oven to 350°F. Spray a 9-inch springform pan with nonstick cooking spray, then dust with flour, knocking out the excess.

In a small bowl, whisk together the flour, cinnamon, cloves, pepper, and salt. In a medium bowl, whisk together the molasses, 1 cup of the sugar, the oil, and the ginger.

In a small saucepan, bring 1 cup water to a boil over high heat. Add the baking soda and stir until dissolved, about 30 seconds. Pour the hot water into the molasses mixture and whisk to mix well. Add the eggs and again whisk to mix well. Finally, stir in the flour mixture until fully blended. Scrape the batter into the prepared pan and smooth the surface with a rubber spatula. Let rest for 10 minutes.

Bake the cake until it springs back from the edges of the pan and a wooden skewer inserted into the center comes out clean, 45 to 60 minutes.

While the cake is baking, halve and pit the plums and chop into ¼-inch pieces. Transfer to a medium bowl, add the remaining 2 tablespoons sugar, and toss to coat evenly. Cover and refrigerate, stirring occasionally, for at least 30 minutes or up to overnight.

Transfer the cake to a wire rack and let cool for 15 minutes. Release the pan sides and lift them off. Using a wide offset spatula, lift the cake from the pan bottom to a serving plate.

To serve, cut the cake into wedges and serve each wedge topped with the plum mixture. (The cake will keep in an airtight container at room temperature for up to 4 days.)

FRESHLY BAKED

Anyone who has stayed at Nick's Cove knows how special it is the moment the breakfast tray arrives. You hear the knock on the door and you open it to a gentleman with a smiling face.

He arrives carrying a tray laden with fresh fruit, scones and muffins warm from the oven, hot coffee, and fresh juice. After setting the tray on your table, he slowly and steadily depresses the plunger of the French press,

releasing a perfect pot of coffee. This is what it's like to wake up at Nick's Cove. It's not just the heated bathroom floors, the wonderfully soft sheets, the sounds of the bay, the beauty of nature, and the peacefulness of watching birds landing on the water. It's also the warmth of someone delivering a daily newspaper, house-made baked goods, and a smile!

I have always wanted Nick's Cove to be known for a few things: signature dishes, annual Santa visits, our s'mores kits, and our scones and muffins. After many iterations, pastry chefs, and a lot of sweet time, we are sharing with you the recipes for our scones and muffins—recipes of which I am especially proud! When you make them for your own breakfast, I am certain you will feel as though you have brought a piece of Nick's Cove home with you.

NICK'S BREAKFAST MUFFINS

2 cups all-purpose flour

2 teaspoons ground cinnamon

2 teaspoons baking powder

½ teaspoon baking soda

½ cup unsalted butter, at room temperature

1 cup sugar

½ teaspoon kosher salt

2 large eggs

¾ cup sour cream

2 tablespoons whole milk

1 teaspoon pure vanilla extract

1 cup dried golden raisins

Makes 12 muffins

Each and every morning at Nick's Cove, we deliver fresh muffins and scones to our cottage guests as part of our complimentary breakfast (along with fresh fruit and juice, tea, and coffee). These breakfast muffins can be made using any dried fruits. In this version, we use golden raisins and plenty of cinnamon, but feel free to experiment with other dried fruits like chopped apples, apricots, cherries, or cranberries (we would suggest omitting the cinnamon if using apricots or cranberries). We use silicone muffin molds for our muffins, placed directly into a standard muffin tin, but you may also use paper muffin liners.

Preheat the oven to 350°F. Line a 12-cup muffin pan with silicone muffin molds or paper liners. If using the silicone molds, spray with nonstick cooking spray. Or spray the muffin pan with cooking spray.

In a small bowl, sift together the flour, cinnamon, baking powder, and baking soda. In a stand mixer fitted with the paddle attachment, beat together the butter, sugar, and salt on medium speed until fluffy and smooth, 3 to 4 minutes. Add the eggs, one at a time, beating well and scraping down the sides of the bowl after each addition. Add the sour cream, milk, and vanilla, and mix on low speed until fully combined. With the mixer on low speed, add the flour mixture in two or three additions, beating well and scraping down the sides of the bowl after each addition. Stir the golden raisins into the batter.

Divide the batter evenly among the muffin cups. Bake, rotating the pan halfway through baking, until the tops are golden brown and a toothpick inserted into the center of a muffin comes out clean, about 18 minutes. Transfer to a wire rack and let cool slightly before serving.

CRANBERRY-ORANGE SCONES

⅔ cup cold buttermilk
  or sour cream
½ cup cold heavy cream
1 teaspoon pure vanilla extract
1 tablespoon finely grated
  orange zest
2¼ cups all-purpose flour
⅓ cup plus 1 tablespoon sugar
1 tablespoon baking powder
2 teaspoons kosher salt
½ teaspoon baking soda
4 tablespoons cold unsalted butter,
  cut into ½-inch cubes
1 cup dried cranberries
About 3 tablespoons turbinado
  sugar (optional)

Makes 1 dozen large or 2 dozen
  small scones

These tender scones are a favorite of our morning guests, and perfect with a cup of tea any time of day. We add plenty of tangy dried cranberries and orange zest, but you could swap out other dried fruits and citrus zest. Dried blueberries and lemon zest would be a great pairing! We generally serve small-size scones, but if you like, you can make large versions, just increase the cooking time by 5 minutes.

In a bowl, whisk together the buttermilk, cream, vanilla, and orange zest. In the bowl of a stand mixer fitted with the paddle attachment, stir together the flour, sugar, baking powder, salt, and baking soda on low speed until combined. Add the cubed butter and mix on low speed until the mixture is crumbly and resembles fresh bread crumbs, with small pieces of butter still visible, 5 to 8 minutes. Add the buttermilk mixture to the flour mixture and mix on low speed just until the dough is evenly moistened. Add the cranberries and mix on low speed until the dough is fully combined; do not overmix.

Transfer the dough to a large piece of parchment paper dusted with flour. Using a rolling pin, roll out the dough into a 9-by-12-inch rectangle that is ¾ to 1 inch thick. Use a large, sharp knife to cut the dough into twelve 3-inch squares. Leave as is for large scones, or cut the squares in half diagonally for small scones.

Slide the parchment and scone dough onto a large sheet pan. Cover the scones with another piece of parchment. Refrigerate for at least 30 minutes or up to 2 days before baking. (The scones can be wrapped in plastic wrap and placed in a freezer bag for up to 1 week; defrost in the refrigerator before baking.)

Preheat the oven to 325°F. Remove the top piece of parchment and space the scones 1 inch apart on the parchment-lined sheet pan. Sprinkle evenly with the turbinado sugar, if using. Bake the scones, rotating the pan halfway through baking, until golden brown and cooked through, about 15 minutes for small scones and about 20 minutes for large scones. Transfer to a wire rack and let cool slightly before serving.

BLONDIE SUNDAES

WITH CANDIED PECANS AND CARAMEL SAUCE

For the candied pecans:
1 tablespoon egg white
1 tablespoon granulated sugar
1 cup pecan or walnut pieces

For the caramel sauce:
1 cup packed light brown sugar
½ cup unsalted butter, cut into cubes
1 teaspoon kosher salt
¼ cup heavy cream
1 teaspoon pure vanilla extract

For the blondies:
1 cup all-purpose flour
1 teaspoon baking powder
½ teaspoon baking soda
1 cup unsalted butter, cut into cubes
2 cups packed light brown sugar
2 large eggs
1½ teaspoons pure vanilla extract
1 cup (6 oz) semisweet chocolate
  chips

For the whipped cream:
¾ cup heavy cream
3 tablespoons powdered sugar
½ teaspoon pure vanilla extract

3 pints vanilla ice cream

Makes 6 servings

Chewy and dense, our blondies are the perfect base for this sky-high ice-cream sundae, which we top with homemade caramel sauce and candied pecans. Want to elevate your dessert game for that next big family gathering? Make two batches of blondies and a double batch each of the sauce and pecans and serve this crowd-pleaser to a raucous round of applause.

To make the candied pecans, preheat the oven to 350°F. Line a sheet pan with parchment paper. In a medium bowl, whisk the egg white until bubbles start to form, about 2 minutes. Add the sugar and whisk to combine. Add the pecans and toss and stir to coat evenly. Pour the pecans onto the prepared pan and spread them in a single layer so they are touching as little as possible.

Bake the pecans, stirring them once about halfway through baking, until toasted and fragrant, about 15 minutes. Let cool on the pan on a wire rack to room temperature. (The candied pecans will keep in an airtight container at room temperature for up to 2 days.)

To make the caramel, in a heavy medium saucepan, combine the brown sugar, butter, and salt over medium-high heat and bring to a gentle boil, stirring to blend. Cook, stirring occasionally, until thickened and the mixture begins to turn a rich dark brown, about 5 minutes. Remove from the heat. While stirring vigorously, add the cream, and then continue to stir until a smooth, silky sauce develops, about 2 minutes. Whisk in the vanilla and set aside. (The caramel can be cooled and stored in an airtight container in the refrigerator for up to 3 days.)

To make the blondies, preheat the oven to 325°F. Spray a 9-inch square baking dish with nonstick cooking spray, then line the bottom with parchment paper.

In a medium bowl, stir together the flour, baking powder, and baking soda. In a large, heavy pot, melt the butter over medium heat, stirring occasionally, until it begins to brown, about 10 minutes. Remove from the heat, add the brown sugar, and stir until well mixed. Add the eggs, one at a time, whisking after each egg until fully blended, then whisk in the vanilla. Add the flour mixture and stir until fully incorporated. Let the mixture cool to room temperature, then stir in the chocolate chips. Pour the batter into the prepared baking dish.

continued . . .

Bake the blondies, rotating the pan back to front about halfway through baking, until golden brown and a toothpick inserted into the center comes out clean, about 25 minutes. Let cool in the pan on a wire rack for at least 30 minutes. Cut into 6 equal pieces and set aside at room temperature. (The blondies will keep in an airtight container at room temperature for up to 3 days.)

To make the whipped cream, in a medium bowl, whisk together the cream, powdered sugar, and vanilla until medium-firm peaks form. Do not overwhip. Cover and refrigerate until ready to use or up to 4 hours.

For each sundae, place a blondie in an individual bowl. Top with 2 generous scoops of ice cream and drizzle the ice cream with 2 tablespoons of the caramel. Top with a big spoonful of whipped cream and finish with a generous 2 tablespoons of the candied pecans. Enjoy right away!

APRICOT ALMOND TART

For the pastry:
½ cup plus 1 tablespoon unsalted
 butter, melted
½ cup sugar
¼ teaspoon pure almond extract
1¼ cups plus 1 tablespoon
 all-purpose flour
½ teaspoon kosher salt
2 tablespoons superfine almond flour

For the filling:
6 apricots, pitted and sliced
 ¼ inch thick
¼ cup sugar
½ cup apricot jam
2 tablespoons warm water
1 tablespoon honey
¼ cup sliced almonds, toasted

Vanilla ice cream, for serving
 (optional)

Makes 6 servings

Maybe it's partly the short season that makes apricots so special. What I do know is that I love them in just about any form: fresh, dried, baked, candied, in jam and chutney. This simple tart with its topping of toasted sliced almonds is one of my favorite apricot recipes. Once you taste its crisp, savory crust and sweet-tart fruit filling, it will quickly become one of your go-to summer desserts.

To make the pastry, preheat the oven to 350°F. Brush the bottom and sides of a 9-inch fluted tart pan with a removable bottom with 1 tablespoon of the melted butter.

In a medium bowl, using a wooden spoon, stir together the remaining ½ cup melted butter, the sugar, and the almond extract until well blended. Add the all-purpose flour and salt and stir until a soft dough forms.

Transfer the dough to the center of the prepared pan and, using your fingertips, evenly press the dough over the bottom and up the sides of the pan. Using fork tines, poke holes into the dough, spacing them about 1½ inches apart.

Bake the dough until set and slightly puffy, 12 to 15 minutes. Transfer the pan to a wire rack and immediately sprinkle the almond flour evenly over the bottom of the tart shell. Set aside while you make the filling. Leave the oven on.

To make the filling, in a medium bowl, toss the apricots with the sugar, coating evenly. Set aside for 10 minutes.

Transfer the apricot mixture to the tart shell and spread in an even layer. Place the tart pan on a large sheet pan. Bake the tart, rotating the pan back to front halfway through baking, until the edges of the crust are golden brown and the fruit is bubbling, 35 to 40 minutes.

Transfer the tart to a wire rack. In a small bowl, whisk together the jam, warm water, and honey until smooth to make a glaze. Using a pastry brush, gently brush the glaze over the apricot filling while the tart is still warm. Sprinkle the almonds evenly over the top.

Set the tart pan on an overturned bowl and carefully slide the ring down. Using a wide offset spatula, lift the tart from the pan bottom to a serving plate. Serve warm or at room temperature, accompanied with ice cream, if desired.

NICK'S IT

For the oatmeal cookies:
2 large eggs
1 teaspoon pure vanilla extract
3 cups old-fashioned rolled oats
1½ cups all-purpose flour
2 teaspoons baking soda
1 teaspoon freshly grated nutmeg
1 teaspoon ground cinnamon
7 tablespoons unsalted butter,
  at room temperature
1 cup granulated sugar
1 cup packed light brown sugar

1½ pints vanilla ice cream
1 lb semisweet chocolate, chopped
¼ cup canola oil

Makes 6 ice cream sandwiches

In 2011, we launched our kids' menu with drawings, puzzles, and a word search and made it large enough to serve as both entertainment and a place mat. Happy kids mean happy parents! It was important to offer healthy—and yummy—food options that our younger guests would enjoy. For dessert, I wanted something fun. Growing up, my favorite treat was San Francisco's It's-It, a chocolate-dipped ice-cream sandwich of vanilla ice cream sandwiched between two big oatmeal cookies, so we decided to make our own version. When it debuted on the kids' menu, we had so many adults requesting it that we moved it to the regular dessert menu.

To make the cookies, in a small bowl, whisk together the eggs and vanilla until blended. In a medium bowl, whisk together the oats, flour, baking soda, nutmeg, and cinnamon.

In a stand mixer fitted with the paddle attachment, beat together the butter and both sugars on medium speed until fluffy and smooth, 5 to 7 minutes. Add the egg mixture in three additions, beating well and scraping down the sides of the bowl after each addition. With the mixer on low speed, add the flour mixture in three additions, beating well and scraping down the sides of the bowl after each addition. Continue to mix until the dough is fully combined, about 1 minute longer.

Transfer the dough to a sheet of plastic wrap and form it into a log that is 1½ inches in diameter. Wrap tightly in the plastic wrap and refrigerate until well chilled, at least 8 hours or up to 1 day in advance.

When you are ready to bake, preheat the oven to 325°F. Line a large sheet pan with parchment paper. Remove the dough from the plastic wrap and cut into 12 equal slices. Using your hands, roll each slice into a ball. Arrange on the prepared sheet pan, spacing the dough balls about 4 inches apart. Using your palm, gently flatten each dough portion into a disk about 3 inches in diameter.

Bake the cookies, rotating the pan back to front once halfway through baking, until golden brown but still soft, about 9 minutes. Transfer to a wire rack and let cool completely.

To assemble the sandwiches, let the ice cream sit at room temperature for about 10 minutes to soften slightly. While the ice cream softens, line a small sheet pan with parchment paper. Arrange half of the cookies, bottom side up on the prepared pan. Fill a small bowl with warm water and place it next to the ice cream.

continued . . .

For each sandwich, dip a large ice cream scoop into the water then scoop ½ cup ice cream and place it on a cookie base. Place another cookie, bottom side down, on top and press gently to spread the ice cream as evenly as possible between the cookies; the ice cream should be about 1 inch thick. Repeat with the remaining cookies and ice cream. Immediately transfer the pan to the freezer and freeze the sandwiches until firm, at least 2 hours or up to overnight.

Pour water to a depth of about 2 inches into a medium saucepan and bring to a gentle simmer over medium-low heat. Rest a heatproof medium bowl on top of the saucepan over (not touching) the water and put the chocolate and oil into the bowl. Heat, stirring often, until the chocolate is mostly melted with only a few pieces remaining. Remove the bowl from the heat and wipe the outside of the bowl dry. The chocolate should be warm but not hot.

Dip each ice-cream sandwich vertically halfway into the chocolate, then return it to the sheet pan. When all the sandwiches are dipped, return the sheet pan to the freezer and freeze until the chocolate hardens, 30 to 60 minutes, then serve. If you will not be eating them right away, wrap each ice cream sandwich in plastic wrap, slip them into a zippered plastic bag or two, and store them flat in the freezer for up to 5 days.

BROWNIE CUPCAKES
WITH BUTTERSCOTCH FROSTING

For the cupcakes:

6 tablespoons unsalted butter, cut into several pieces

8 oz bittersweet chocolate (70 percent cacao), coarsely chopped

3 large eggs

1 cup granulated sugar

¼ teaspoon kosher salt

1 teaspoon pure vanilla extract

⅓ cup plus 1 tablespoon all-purpose flour

For the butterscotch frosting:

1 cup (6 oz) butterscotch chips

8 oz cream cheese, at room temperature

6 tablespoons unsalted butter, at room temperature

1 cup powdered sugar, sifted

2 tablespoons heavy cream

½ teaspoon pure vanilla extract

Makes 12 cupcakes

Easy to make and over-the-top creamy and delicious, this luscious butterscotch frosting can be used on nearly any type of cake, cupcake, or sandwich cookie. But it tastes especially amazing on these wonderfully dense brownie cupcakes. Bake them once for your friends or family and be prepared to be asked to make them again and again.

Preheat the oven to 350°F. Spray a 12-cup muffin pan with nonstick cooking spray.

To make the cupcakes, pour water to a depth of about 2 inches into a medium saucepan and bring to a gentle simmer over medium-low heat. Rest a heatproof medium bowl on top of the saucepan over (not touching) the water. Add the butter and chocolate to the bowl and heat, stirring often, until the butter and chocolate are melted and the mixture is smooth. Remove from heat and set aside to cool slightly, about 10 minutes.

In a medium bowl, beat together the eggs and granulated sugar until light and fluffy, about 2 minutes. Add the melted chocolate mixture, salt, and vanilla and whisk until smooth, then fold in the flour until fully incorporated and no white streaks remain.

Divide the batter evenly among the muffin cups. Bake until a toothpick inserted into the center of a cupcake or two comes out clean, 20 to 25 minutes. Transfer to a wire rack and let cool completely.

To make the frosting, once again set up a heatproof medium bowl over (not touching) simmering water in a saucepan, put the butterscotch chips in the bowl, and heat, stirring often, until melted and smooth. Remove from the heat and let cool to room temperature.

In a stand mixer fitted with the paddle attachment, beat the cream cheese on medium-high speed until smooth, about 2 minutes. Add the butter and powdered sugar and beat until well mixed, about 2 minutes. Add the melted butterscotch chips, cream, and vanilla and beat until blended, about 2 minutes longer.

When the cupcakes have cooled, turn them out of the pan and arrange them upright on a work surface. Using an icing spatula or a piping bag fitted with a small plain or star tip, frost the cupcakes with the frosting.

Serve the cupcakes right away, or store in an airtight container in the refrigerator for up to 3 days.

BITTERSWEET CHOCOLATE TORTE

For the torte:

12 oz bittersweet or semisweet
  chocolate, coarsely chopped
¾ cup unsalted butter, cut
  into pieces
6 large eggs
¾ cup sugar
2 teaspoons pure vanilla extract

For the glaze:

½ cup heavy cream
½ cup dark corn syrup
9 oz bittersweet or semisweet
  chocolate, finely chopped

2 tablespoons bittersweet or
  semisweet chocolate shavings
Sliced fresh strawberries or
  raspberries for serving (optional)

Makes 6 servings

This ultrarich chocolate torte is dense, moist, and exceedingly delicious. It gets its loft from beaten egg whites, so be sure the bowl and beaters you use for whipping are perfectly clean or the egg whites will not rise to their full potential. Also, be gentle when you fold the beaten whites into the chocolate mixture or their light, airy structure will collapse. Taking this extra care at each step will be rewarded at the table.

To make the torte, preheat the oven to 350°F. Butter a 9-inch springform pan. Line the bottom of the pan with parchment paper, then butter the paper. Wrap the outside of the pan with aluminum foil.

In a heavy medium saucepan over low heat, combine the chocolate and butter and heat, stirring often, until melted and smooth. Remove from the heat and let cool to lukewarm, stirring often.

In a large bowl, using an electric mixer, beat together the eggs, sugar, and vanilla on medium-high speed until very thick and pale, 5 to 8 minutes. Using a rubber spatula, fold the lukewarm chocolate mixture into the egg mixture just until combined. Pour the batter into the prepared pan.

Bake the torte until the top is puffed and cracked and a wooden skewer inserted into the center comes out with some moist crumbs attached, about 35 minutes. Let cool completely in the pan on a wire rack (the top will fall).

Gently press down on the crusty top to even the surface of the torte. Slide a small, thin-bladed knife along the inside of the pan to loosen the torte sides. Release the pan sides and lift them off. Place a 9-inch tart pan bottom or cardboard round on top of the torte and invert the torte. Lift off the springform pan bottom and peel off the parchment.

For the glaze, in a medium saucepan, combine the cream and corn syrup over medium heat and bring to a simmer, about 4 minutes. Remove from the heat. Add the chocolate and whisk gently until melted and smooth.

Put a wire rack on a sheet pan. Set the torte on the rack. Using an icing spatula, spread about ½ cup of the glaze smoothly over the top and sides of the torte.

Place the sheet pan into the freezer and freeze until the glaze is almost set, about 3 minutes. Pour the remaining glaze over the cake, smoothing the top and sides with the spatula. Using a wide offset spatula, lift the torte from the pan bottom or cardboard round to a serving plate and refrigerate the torte until the glaze is firm, about 1 hour. (The torte can be made up to 1 day in advance of serving, covered with a cake dome, and stored at room temperature.)

Garnish with the chocolate shavings and strawberries (if using), and serve at room temperature.

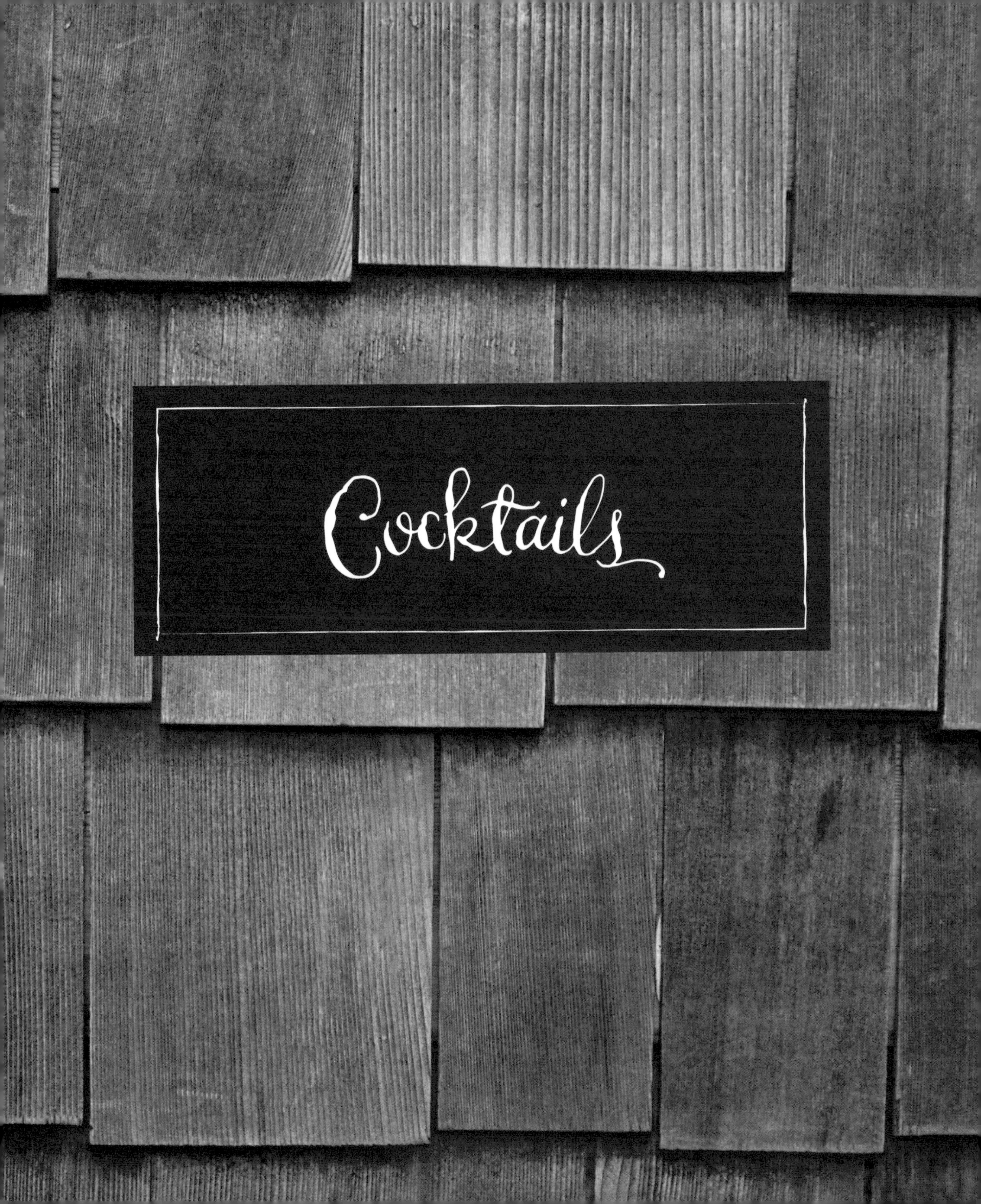
Cocktails

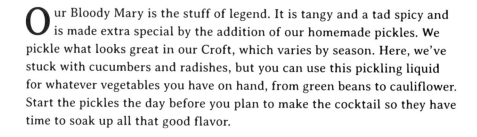

NICK'S BLOODY MARY

For the pickles:

2 cups Champagne vinegar

2 tablespoons sugar

2 tablespoons kosher salt

1 jalapeño chile, seeded and sliced

1 teaspoon red pepper flakes

6 assorted radishes, trimmed and
   sliced into ¼-inch-thick rounds

1 Kirby cucumber, cut lengthwise
   into 12 spears

For the Bloody Mary mix:

⅛ teaspoon red pepper flakes

⅛ teaspoon ground cumin

⅛ teaspoon ground coriander

⅛ teaspoon celery seeds

⅛ teaspoon black peppercorns

1 (46-oz) can tomato juice

Juice of 3 lemons

2 tablespoons Worcestershire sauce

2 teaspoons prepared horseradish

2 bay leaves

Kosher salt

12 oz high-quality vodka (such as
   Hangar 1)

Ice cubes

Vinegar-based hot sauce

6 pimento-stuffed green olives

6 cocktail onions

6 lemon wedges

Freshly ground black pepper

Makes 6 cocktails

Our Bloody Mary is the stuff of legend. It is tangy and a tad spicy and is made extra special by the addition of our homemade pickles. We pickle what looks great in our Croft, which varies by season. Here, we've stuck with cucumbers and radishes, but you can use this pickling liquid for whatever vegetables you have on hand, from green beans to cauliflower. Start the pickles the day before you plan to make the cocktail so they have time to soak up all that good flavor.

To make the pickles, in a medium saucepan, combine the vinegar, 1½ cups water, the sugar, salt, chile, and pepper flakes over medium heat and bring to a boil. Reduce the heat to medium-low and simmer gently until the sugar and salt have dissolved and the mixture is fragrant, 8 to 10 minutes. Remove from the heat and let cool completely, then transfer to an airtight container large enough to hold both the liquid and the vegetables. Refrigerate until cold, about 1 hour.

Add the radish slices and cucumber spears to the cold pickling liquid, making sure they are fully immersed, and refrigerate for at least 8 hours or up to 1 month before serving.

To make the Bloody Mary mix, in a spice grinder, combine the pepper flakes, cumin, coriander, celery seeds, and peppercorns and process to a fine powder. Pour the tomato juice into a large glass pitcher, add the spice mixture, lemon juice, Worcestershire sauce, and horseradish, and stir to mix well. Add the bay leaves, then season to taste with salt. Cover and refrigerate until ready to use or up to 5 days.

To make the cocktails, have ready six pint-size glasses. Add 2 oz of the vodka to each glass, then fill the glasses with ice cubes. Pour in the Bloody Mary mix to nearly fill each glass (about 5 oz/⅔ cup), then add a dash or two of hot sauce to each glass. For each cocktail, spear an olive, 2 slices pickled radish, and an onion with a bamboo spear, then add to the glass. Add a lemon wedge to the rim of the glass, then add 2 pickled cucumber spears to the glass. Grind a little black pepper over the top and serve.

TOMALES BAY GIN AND TONIC

WITH HOMEMADE TONIC SYRUP

For the tonic syrup:

1½ cups agave syrup

¼ cup cinchona powder

3 tablespoons citric acid, or
  ½ cup fresh lemon juice

Grated zest of 2 limes

Grated zest of 1 lemon

4 allspice berries

1 cardamom pod

For the cocktails:

4 oz gin (such as Uncle Val's)

Ice cubes

2 oz tonic syrup (above)

Juice of 2 limes

8 oz soda water

2 lime wedges

Makes 2 cocktails

A t Nick's Cove, the bar staff enjoys taking the classics and "Nick'ing" them up with house-made syrups and interesting herbs. If you aren't typically a fan of G&Ts, try this one and we think you'll be converted. Making your own tonic syrup not only yields a more flavorful cocktail but will also elicit kudos from your family and friends. Earthen-colored cinchona bark is a natural source of quinine and is available online (we like the Penn Herb Company, found at pennherb.com) and in well-stocked markets. You can buy either the bark and grind it yourself or use the powder. Our homemade tonic syrup pairs perfectly with the floral notes of locally made Uncle Val's small-batch botanical gin, but you can use your favorite gin or even vodka if you like.

To make the tonic syrup, in a medium saucepan, stir together 2 cups water, the agave syrup, cinchona powder, citric acid, lime and lemon zests, allspice berries, and cardamom over medium heat and bring to a boil. Reduce the heat to low and simmer until reduced by half, 15 to 20 minutes. Remove from the heat and let cool completely. Strain through a fine-mesh sieve into an airtight container; discard the solids. You should have about 3 cups. Refrigerate the syrup until ready to use or for up to 1 month.

To make the cocktails, have ready two rocks glasses. Put 2 oz of the gin into each glass, then fill the glasses with ice cubes. Add 1 oz of the tonic syrup, the juice of 1 lime, and 4 oz of the soda water to each glass and stir well. Garnish each cocktail with a lime wedge and serve.

KEEP IT FRESH

Gin and tonics are the perfect drink to show off your herb garden. Try experimenting by adding different aromatic herbs, like a sprig of fresh rosemary, thyme, or mint, as well as other colorful or fragrant ingredients, like citrus peel, edible flowers, and slices of cucumber.

MOSCOW MULE

WITH GINGER-LEMONGRASS SYRUP

For the ginger-lemongrass syrup:
8 oz fresh ginger, peeled and
  roughly chopped
1½ cups agave syrup
3 tablespoons citric acid, or
  ⅓ cup fresh lemon juice
½ cup chopped fresh lemongrass
  (bulb portion only, with tough
  outer leaves discarded)
Grated zest of 3 limes

For the cocktails:
4 oz vodka (such as Hangar 1)
About 1½ cups crushed ice
3 oz ginger syrup (above)
8 oz club soda
Juice of 1 lime
4 dashes of Angostura bitters
½ lime, cut into 2 wedges

Makes 2 cocktails

What sets our Moscow Mule apart is our spicy homemade ginger syrup, which packs a punch while not overpowering the other ingredients. Grown in our Croft, the lemongrass we add to the ginger syrup delivers the perfect herbal-citrus accent to this popular cocktail. Made from locally distilled vodka, fresh lime juice, bitters, and our ginger syrup, all this beauty needs is a splash of club soda to make it the mule it is. We serve our mules in copper mugs, which are traditional, but you can use whatever mugs or glasses you like.

To make the ginger syrup, in a blender, combine the ginger and 2 cups water and blend on high speed to a smooth puree. Transfer the puree to a small saucepan, add 1 cup water, the agave syrup, citric acid, lemongrass, and lime zest, and stir to combine. Place over medium heat and bring to a simmer. Adjust the heat to maintain a steady simmer and cook, stirring occasionally, until the mixture begins to reduce and become syrupy, about 15 minutes. Strain through a fine-mesh sieve into an airtight container; discard the solids. You should have about 3 cups. Let cool to room temperature, then refrigerate until ready to use or up to 1 week.

To make the cocktails, have ready two copper mugs or other cocktail glasses. Put 2 oz of the vodka into each mug, then fill the mugs with ice. Add 1½ oz of the ginger syrup, 4 oz of the club soda, half of the lime juice, and 2 dashes of the bitters to each mug. Stir each cocktail once, then garnish with a lime wedge and serve.

MIX IT UP

Swap out the vodka in this cocktail for bourbon to make a Kentucky Mule. Add an ounce of maple syrup to the bourbon version and you have a delightful Nor'easter. Substitute rum for the vodka and you've made a Dark n' Stormy. All of these cocktails are best when shared with friends.

LOCAL SPIRITS

Lucky for us, small-batch spirit makers have popped up all around Sonoma, Marin, and Napa Counties, making it easy for us to maintain our menu of handcrafted cocktails.

In keeping with our mission of using the best local products we can find, all of the cocktails found on our menu use locally made spirits. The difficulty for us is that there are so many good ones nearby. At any given

time, you can find our handcrafted cocktails making good use of products from St. George Spirits, Griffo Distillery, Spirit Works Distillery, Hanson of Sonoma Distillery, Prohibition Spirits, Uncle Val's, and Barber Lee Spirits.

But we don't stick only to local spirits. We also use small-batch bitters from Bitter Girl Bitters and FloraLuna Bitters, both based in Sonoma County. In the early days of her company, the founder of Bitter Girl Bitters, Erin Elizabeth Hines, worked behind the bar at Nick's Cove,

which means we very well could have been the first to use her bitters.

Our bar crew is a very creative group, and we encourage them to test out their latest concoctions at work. This philosophy has led to our very own tonic syrup made from cinchona bark, ginger syrup for our version of the Moscow Mule, and the delicious stout syrup that we use in the Nick's Cove Marshall Manhattan.

MARSHALL MANHATTAN

WITH SPICED STOUT SYRUP

For the spiced stout syrup:
12 oz stout (such as Anderson Valley
   oatmeal stout)
½ cup sugar
Finely grated zest and juice
   of ½ lemon
2 whole cloves
1 cinnamon stick
¼ teaspoon ground allspice

Ice cubes
4 oz bourbon
1½ oz spiced stout syrup (above)
2 dashes of Angostura bitters
4 spiced or brandied cherries

Makes 2 cocktails

O ur Marshall Manhattan is based on the classic but with the addition of winter spices. We replaced the sweet vermouth with a flavorful house-made stout reduction. We like using Anderson Valley oatmeal stout because it has warm, toasty notes that are ideal on a foggy night at Nick's Cove. The rich, complex flavors of this inspired drink will both please the palate at the moment of sipping and leave a lasting impression that you'll recall at your next cocktail hour.

To make the syrup, in a saucepan, stir together the beer, sugar, lemon zest and juice, cloves, cinnamon stick, and allspice over medium heat and bring to a simmer. Reduce the heat to medium-low to maintain a gentle simmer and cook, stirring occasionally, until reduced by about half, about 20 minutes. Remove from the heat and let cool completely. Strain through a fine-mesh sieve into an airtight container; discard the solids. You should have about 2 cups. Refrigerate the syrup until ready to use or up to 2 months.

To make the cocktails, have ready two chilled martini glasses. Fill a mixing glass with ice cubes. Add the bourbon, stout syrup, and bitters and stir with a barspoon until cold, 15 to 30 seconds. Strain into the chilled glasses. Garnish each cocktail with two cherries speared onto a pick, then serve.

BARTENDER'S TIP

There are so many delicious styles of stouts that would be awesome to try in this recipe. A milk stout might lend creamy sweetness, an oyster stout could add an element of salinity, and a coffee stout might add chocolaty, bittersweet notes.

AUTUMN CROFT COCKTAIL

WITH ROSE GERANIUM–NASTURTIUM SYRUP

For the rose geranium–nasturtium syrup:

1 cup boiling water

1 cup sugar

8 rose geranium buds

3 nasturtium flowers

3 oz pisco (such as Caravedo brand)

1½ oz rose geranium–nasturtium syrup (above)

1½ oz almond-flavored crème liqueur (such as Tempus Fugit Crème de Noyaux)

Juice of 2 lemons

4 dashes of orange bitters

Ice cubes

2 orange twists

Makes 2 cocktails

This cocktail is an homage to our garden. Every season, we change up the ingredients depending on which herbs, flowers, and vegetables are growing in the Croft. At the time of writing, our Croft cocktail consisted of a house-made rose geranium–nasturtium syrup, Tempus Fugit Crème de Noyaux, pisco (brandy), lemon juice, and orange bitters. The resulting cocktail is a beautiful pink color but still feels autumnal because of its nutty and citrusy elements.

To make the syrup, in a heatproof medium bowl, stir together the boiling water, sugar, rose geranium buds, and nasturtiums until the sugar dissolves. Set aside to steep for about 2 hours. Strain through a fine-mesh sieve into an airtight container; discard the solids. You should have 1½ cups. Refrigerate until ready to use or up to 1 week.

To make the cocktails, have ready two chilled coupes. In a cocktail shaker combine the pisco, rose geranium–nasturtium syrup, liqueur, lemon juice, and bitters. Fill the shaker with ice, cover, and shake vigorously for about 20 seconds. Strain into the glasses, garnish each cocktail with an orange twist, and serve.

Legend of the Bootlegger

Bootlegging in Marin and Sonoma Counties has been widely written about, and resident old-timers like to tell their stories of what they witnessed during Prohibition. From what I have read and heard from local ranchers and dairymen, Tomales, Marshall, and elsewhere in West Marin all had their share of Prohibition secrets.

With dairymen renting a piece of their land for clandestine distilleries and hundreds of cases of Canadian whisky regularly arriving by boat at night, where they were off-loaded to waiting cars for transport, Tomales Bay definitely played a significant local role in the bootlegging business during Prohibition.

Some of the spirits made in these unlawful distilleries were whisked off to speakeasies hidden in friends' homes in Petaluma, just twenty-five miles east. Some likely stayed nearby for local consumption.

During a visit with Judi (Matkovich) Ritz, she confirmed the rumors that Nick Kojich had indeed been a local boot-legger. The story goes that one morning while fishing in Tomales Bay, Nick and his brothers-in-law pulled up what they thought was a heavy herring catch only to find a line of Canadian whisky. According to Judi, it was at that moment that Nick hatched the idea to bootleg. The original Nick's Cove building was two stories, so Nick would simply give three small taps to the ceiling when authorities came in to quiet down the production going on upstairs. The booze was stored alongside the glass buoys in the basement of what are now the cottages Fly Fisherman and Uncle Andy's.

Although the days of basement speakeasies and illicit distilleries are long gone, in some ways our early twentieth-century history has come full circle: those illegal small-batch distilleries of the past were wildly popular, and today we are just as enthusiastic about the many small-batch distilleries that are now flourishing in the area (see page 176).

Sonoma County detective John Pemberton and unnamed federal agents raid an illegal still in Sonoma County in the 1920s.

ACKNOWLEDGMENTS

Even though this book has been my passion project for many years, it couldn't have happened without the extraordinary effort of the team behind it. First and foremost, a heartfelt thank you to my PR consultant, friend, and fellow ginger mamma, Caitlin Sandberg Brancale of Poppyseed PR. Caitlin painstakingly held my (and everyone's) hand through each marketing meeting, book meeting, photoshoot, and "offline" call, helping keep us all on track. She is a rock star in so many ways, and I could not have done this without her.

A huge thank you to our dedicated and humble executive chef Kua Speer, who took recipes that ranged from our reopening in 2007 through numerous talented chefs, all the way to his current additions on our menu. Kua carved out many additional hours from his already busy schedule to ensure the recipes were written accurately, tested for the home cook, and camera-ready for their beauty shots.

Words cannot describe how grateful I am for our amazing photographer, Frankie Frankeny, who truly made my dream come true: to have a book that is both beautiful and timeless. I am grateful for her friendship, her passion, her dedication, and her guidance.

This book would not be in your hands if it were not for the talents of so many people. Thank you to the team at CAMERON + COMPANY— publisher Chris Gruener, executive editor Kim Laidlaw, creative director Iain Morris, and art director Suzi Hutsell—for believing in this project, shepherding it from beginning to end, and creating a design that I believe will resonate with everyone. A heartfelt thank you to our many fabulous recipe testers. And, of course, a sincere thank you to the incredible team at Nick's Cove: Wade Nakamine, Angela Price, Dustin Moore, and the entire staff of the property. Nick's Cove wouldn't be what it is without each and every one of you. Last but certainly not least, a heartfelt thank you to Brendan Thomas, the farmer who brought my vision for the garden to life with his heart and hands.

This is as much a cookbook as it is a historical homage to the amazing people who were behind making Nick's Cove what it is today, from Nick and Frances Kojich and the larger-than-life Ruth and Al Gibson to the visionary chefs Pat Kuleto and Mark Franz. Thank you to Ron and Judi (Matkovich) Ritz for taking the time to help me fill in the blanks. I am thankful beyond measure to the Ashe Family, who were right by my side the entire time as we brought this place into the full glory that it is today.

No endeavor this large can happen without the support of so many and I have two wonderfully supportive people to thank: my husband, Hans, and our son, Bohdan. Thank you for your love and support—the best is yet to come! And, for everything this property is to us, to them, and to you, our guests, thank you for seeing the magic that is Nick's Cove.

INDEX

CAMERON + COMPANY
149 Kentucky Street, Suite 7
Petaluma, California 94952
www.cameronbooks.com

Publisher: *Chris Gruener*
Creative Director: *Iain R. Morris*
Executive Editor: *Kim Laidlaw*
Art Director & Designer: *Suzi Hutsell*
Managing Editor: *Jan Hughes*
Editorial Assistant: *Mason Harper*

Writer: *Dena Grunt*
Recipe Development: *Kua Speer and Caitlin Sandberg*
Photographer: *Frankie Frankeny*
Photographer Assistants: *Audrey Kuhn, Tejas Doshi*
Illustrator: *Nicky Ovitt*

Additional photography by: Erin Wrightsman: 11 • Courtesy of
the California History Room, California State Library, Sacramento,
California: 19 (top left) • Civil war photographs, 1861–1865, Library
of Congress, Prints and Photographs Division: 19 (top right) •
Courtesy, the Sonoma County Library: 19 (bottom right), 44, 183 •
Courtesy, History San José: 20 (top) • Milo Woodbridge Williams
Papers, UC San Diego Library: 20 (bottom left and bottom right) •
Courtesy of Nick's Cove pages 21–25, 108, 124 • Dorothy M. Hill
Collection, Meriam Library Special Collections, California State
University, Chico: 82

Library of Congress Cataloging-in-Publication
Data available.

ISBN: 978-1-944903-65-7

10 9 8 7 6 5 4 3 2 1

Printed in China